1/06
ⓦ

W9-BCJ-282

473. 921

Wuk

Eisenhower

Eisenhower

John Wukovits

Foreword by General Wesley K. Clark

palgrave
macmillan

First published in 2006 by
PALGRAVE MACMILLAN™
175 Fifth Avenue, New York, N.Y. 10010 and
Houndmills, Basingstoke, Hampshire, England RG21 6XS.
Companies and representatives throughout the world.

PALGRAVE MACMILLAN is the global academic imprint of the Palgrave Macmillan division of St. Martin's Press, LLC and of Palgrave Macmillan Ltd. Macmillan® is a registered trademark in the United States, United Kingdom and other countries. Palgrave is a registered trademark in the European Union and other countries.

All photos courtesy of the Dwight D. Eisenhower Library & Museum, Abilene, Kansas.

ISBN-13: 978-1-4039-7137-1
ISBN-10: 1-4039-7137-4

Library of Congress Cataloging-in-Publication Data
Wukovits, John F., 1944–
    Eisenhower/John Wukovits ; and foreword by Wesley K. Clark
        p.   cm.—(Great Generals)
    Includes bibliographic references and index
    ISBN 1-4039-7137-4 (alk. Paper)
    1. Eisenhower, Dwight D. (Dwight David), 1890–1969.   2. Generals—United States—Biography.   3. United States. Army—Biography.   4. Presidents—United States—Biography.   5. World War, 1939–1945—Biography.   6. United States—History, Military—20th century   I. Title   II. Series.
E836.W855   2006
973.921092—dc22
[B]
                    2006043254

A catalogue record of the book is available from the British Library.

Design by Letra Libre

First edition: October 2006
10   9   8   7   6   5   4   3   2   1
Printed in the United States of America.

To my oldest daughter, Amy,
a constant source of
joy and love

Contents

Part IV

Supreme Commander

Part V

After the War

Photosection appears between pages 104 and 105

Foreword

"I LIKE IKE". IT WAS THE POLITICAL SLOGAN THAT CAPTURED America—and won the Presidency—at a time when the United States was facing a dark and uncertain future. Two years into the Korean War, with no end in sight, and a deepening threat of Soviet military action in Europe, Americans sought a proven leader. General Dwight D. Eisenhower was that man.

The slogan was remarkably accurate. Eisenhower was truly likeable. But he was also much, much more. He was a victorious military leader whose sense of duty had transcended his upbringing, his profession, and allowed him to lead an Alliance that won a world war, bringing peace and prosperity to America.

There was always a lot to like about Ike, as John Wukovits demonstrates in this excellent biography. He was the middle brother, third from the oldest. He was capable in school—though not a great intellectual—with a keen sense of justice, a strong character, and the physique to match. When there was a bully to be defeated, his boyhood friends knew that Ike was the man. But mostly, he saw himself as a sportsman. He was a rugged competitor and an outstanding athlete—football was his great love—and a team leader. Ike's large family had few resources, so it was the United States Military Academy at West Point, with its free education and first rate sports teams that pulled him in. And then, as often happens, he was sidelined by injuries. There was nothing left but to complete his studies, graduate, and become a commissioned officer. Like many cadets, Eisenhower was not captivated by West Point academics, but as a young officer he was thrilled by the challenge and opportunities of the service. He worked hard, bonded with his troops, and demonstrated real competence in leadership and management. He won the support, friendship, and respect of just about everyone he served with. And he was a tough taskmaster, deploying into the Army the kinds of no-nonsense leadership he'd first learned in sports. However, Ike didn't get the big breaks early. A year into his service, the United States organized a punitive expedition—really, an invasion—of Mexico. Eisenhower wasn't picked to go along. By the next year, the Army was in full mobilization to go to war in Europe. But Ike never got to battle, unlike many of his West Point classmates. Still, Ike was now "in the hunt," emotionally committed to succeed in the profession of arms, despite his lack of combat record. And it is Ike's personal growth and character that has provided such a powerful legacy for the officer corps. He had incredibly keen instincts for people, but he also proved an apt student, and was a natural leader who grew with every experience.

The years between the end of World War I and the beginning of World War II were frustrating to most everyone associated with the US Army. Money was tight, forces were cut, units deactivated, procurement deferred, training reduced and many of the most important lessons of World War I forgotten. Many officers resigned to pursue other opportunities. Ike didn't. He stayed through the tough years, building relationships, studying, and preparing himself for the future. It is this period, so well described by Wukovits, that gave Ike the professional foundation he needed to succeed in the rapidly expanding and stressful Army at the start of World War II. For it wasn't just that he was well-known and liked, it was his exceptional competence that brought him to the fore. Ike could organize, manage people, and solve problems, everything from disciplinary issues with the troops to big strategic issues. He thought clearly and spoke directly. And these were the skills he needed when he got the Big Job—commanding US forces in the European Theater of Operations. From here on, Ike's public record is well-known, but superficial: he went on the command Operation Overlord, the D-Day invasion of Normandy, led Allied Forces into Germany, and then, after the defeat of Nazi Germany returned home to a hero's welcome and subsequent election as President.

The truth, as John Wukovits tells it, is considerably more complex and interesting. Ike had to build a team of not only US but also British officers, many older and far more experienced than he was. He had to grow through the vagaries and setbacks of war, losing a crucial early battle, and almost losing his job, while he handled the enormous egos of political leaders and military rivals. He suffered isolation and loneliness, deprived of close family, and subjected to a staggering workload, and yet he bore it all with skill, charm, and outward good humor. In the end, Ike was defined, like most generals, by the success of his campaigns. In leading the victory of Allied Command Europe, he had defeated the most competent enemy the United States had ever faced. And yet strangely, he is remembered within the Armed Forces more as a political general than a "warfighter." Perhaps it was because the demands of his job forced him to attend to grand strategy and the interface between the military and political leaders. Perhaps it was because as an Alliance leader he was gracious enough to allow other generals, erstwhile rivals for recognition and advancement, to claim their share of the successes, sometimes at his own expense. Or perhaps it was simply because, with his outgoing personality, warmth and sincerity, he seemed above the rough and tumble, down-in-the-dirt business of leadership in war. But, as John Wukovits makes clear, Ike was every bit the combat general, from his passion for the troops to his ability to make the tough command decisions.

I believe the record shows that had he been merely a division, corps, or army commander, he would have been every bit as successful as any of his rivals. But Ike was required to do and be something more: he was the first of the modern military leaders to operate at the military-political command level. As such he set the standard for all to follow. It's true that he went on to become President, and made key decisions there, too, ending the war in Korea, refraining from joining the French in a futile effort to fight Ho Chi Minh in Indochina, castigating our British and French allies for the 1956 invasion of Egypt, and a host of other great calls. But it was as an Allied Commander that Ike is most worthy of study and emulation. He built relationships of trust and confidence, fostered a remarkable spirit of teamwork, and traded off purely military considerations against the strategic and political in a pragmatic calculus that led to success and also represented the highest form of the military art. These were the remarkable contributions of the man from Abilene, a true American hero, and a lasting inspiration in generalship. And most everyone in America, and much of the world, admired and liked him to boot.

—General Wesley K. Clark

PART I

Preparation and Roots

"Eisenhower's in the Area"

A DIFFICULT TASK FACED FIRST LIEUTENANT WALLACE C. STROBEL as he waited with the men of E Company, at Greenham Common Airfield in England on the evening of June 5, 1944. In the largest amphibious assault ever mounted, he and his advance force of paratroopers would leap into the fields of Normandy, France, that night, seize control of key roads and bridges, and establish the first Allied presence in Western Europe since Adolf Hitler's vaunted German Army churned its way to the English Channel in 1940. Four long years had interceded, years in which the Allies had rebounded from the near-disasters of 1940 with successes in North Africa and Italy. Now, the potent conglomeration of American, British, and Canadian troops faced the moment both Hitler and the Allies had known would one day come—the moment when the Allies would take the fight to mainland Europe and begin the arduous campaign to chase Hitler back into Germany.

Lieutenant Strobel hoped the operation would unfold more smoothly than the weather portended. Heavy winds and rains had lashed the British coast in recent days, but at least the stormy conditions had somewhat abated.

He waited near the tented assembly area for word that their airplane was ready. Like the other young Americans, he had blackened his hands and face with burned cork, cocoa, and cooking oil to avoid being easily detected in the moonlit French night. Unlike the other men, he bore a sign around his neck with the number 23. As jumpmaster of plane number 23 in the 502nd Parachute Infantry Regiment, 101st Airborne Division, Strobel had to make sure the men assigned to that aircraft gathered at the proper location.

A commotion disrupted Strobel's thoughts. "Eisenhower's in the area,"[1] one man shouted, and before long word raced from soldier to soldier that the supreme commander, General Dwight D. Eisenhower, the man responsible for their role in the assault, had dropped by for a visit. Strobel looked down the muddy path to see Eisenhower and a small group of people walking directly toward him.

Eisenhower had had to get out of headquarters. Too many demands and too many high-ranking people had turned his exhausting schedule into a pressure-laden vortex of emotions where anger and tension extinguished optimism and certitude. The strain of the past weeks had been enough to kill a man; the problems never seemed to cease. Eisenhower had faced questions about logistics and the weather; he had sat through countless briefings and meetings; he had tried to patch the tenuous fabric that composed the British-American alliance. Now, as supreme commander, he had just issued orders sending young men into a battle from which many would never return.

Headquarters was not the place he wanted to be. Instead, he hopped into a car with his driver and a solitary staff officer and headed to nearby Newbury, away from the generals and colonels, to be with the privates and the corporals, to be, particularly, with the 101st Airborne and the other airborne units who, if one prediction proved correct, would suffer 70 percent casualties within hours.

Eisenhower's driver, Kay Summersby, wondered how the troops would react to seeing their commander only moments before their departure for battle. "I needn't have worried," she later wrote. "They went crazy, yelling and cheering because 'Ike' had come to see them off."[2]

Instead of addressing the entire assemblage, in more personal fashion, Eisenhower gathered small groups of men about him. Strobel walked toward the general and stopped only feet away.

"[Eisenhower] asked my name and which state I was from," Strobel recounted. When the soldier replied he was from Michigan, Eisenhower said, "Oh yes, Michigan . . . great fishing there . . . been there several times and like it."[3]

Eisenhower asked Strobel if he and his men were ready for the operation and if they had been well briefed. Strobel explained they had been thoroughly trained and each man was prepared to do his duty.

Other troops contributed their evaluations of the coming operation. A sergeant said, "Hell, we ain't worried, General. It's the Krauts that ought to be worrying now." A private chipped in with, "Look out, Hitler, here we come."[4]

Eisenhower grinned and started to unwind. Instead of gripes from subordinates at headquarters or complaints from generals and heads of state, he listened as boys barely out of high school told him not to worry, that everything would be fine.

The moving scene impressed British reporter Goronwy Ross, who was unaccustomed to witnessing a general interact so comfortably with the troops. "General Eisenhower spoke to each of the crews individually, joked with them and almost always asked them where their home was . . ." As Eisenhower moved from group to group, "one was suddenly aware that this general and these men were intimately associated in some great romantic enterprise, whose significance could not be wholly grasped by an Englishman, and yet one felt it to be of profound importance . . ."[5]

A reinvigorated Eisenhower told the troops not to worry about the German air arm. "If you see airplanes overhead, they will be ours,"[6] he reassured them.

Strobel noticed the general appeared calm, cheerful, almost as if by being in the presence of the men, he had received a much-needed jolt of energy. "He chatted a little more, which I believe was intended to relax us and I think that all of us being keyed up and ready to go buoyed him some- what." Eisenhower's surprise visit lifted the men's spirits, but Strobel saw an unexpected effect and concluded it "was [Eisenhower's] morale that was improved by being with such a remarkably 'high' group of troops."[7]

Eisenhower indeed drew strength and reassurance from the men. He always had throughout a military career that had begun 29 years earlier, when he walked out of West Point as a second lieutenant. Privates and cor- porals had a refreshing way of deflating egos and puncturing through the politics to what was important—the men and the plan. The paratroopers' positive demeanor that night was their way of lending approval to the plans Eisenhower helped assemble and their way of indicating that no matter what happened, they believed in him. They were ready. As much as the men drew strength and inspiration from Eisenhower, he drew the same from them in equal measure. Mutual admiration existed between Eisen- hower and the infantry he commanded.

The men then filed toward their aircraft, taking with them that buoy- ancy they had briefly imparted to their commander who would now return to headquarters. "General Eisenhower turned, shoulders sagging, the loneliest man in the world," recalled his driver. "Well, it's on," he told her. Eisenhower then looked to the sky, hoping he had done all he could for those young men, and added, "No one can stop it now."[8]

CHAPTER 1

+‑‑‑=‑‑‑+

"Kansas Isn't the Whole World"

IRONICALLY, DWIGHT EISENHOWER'S ANCESTORS CAME FROM A region of the world whose destruction he would later so capably orchestrate. Family stories reveal that centuries before, Eisenhower's relatives from Bavaria served as medieval warriors for the famed local ruler, Charlemagne. Over the years pacifist tendencies tempered the clan's militaristic leanings to such a degree that in the seventeenth century some, who then spelled the last name Eisenhauer, a word meaning "iron cutter," fled to Switzerland to escape the ravages of the Thirty Years' War.

In 1741 Hans Nicholas Eisenhauer transplanted the family to the New World, moving first to Philadelphia and later settling near present-day Harrisburg. Several Eisenhauer boys served in the Civil War before Dwight's grandfather, the dynamic Reverend Jacob Eisenhower, uprooted his family from Pennsylvania and headed toward the lush prairies of Kansas. He purchased 160 acres of farmland 12 miles south of Abilene, determined to combine a lucrative career in raising corn and breeding animals with his love for delivering thundering sermons.

Jacob's interests did not extend to his son, David, born in 1863. Quiet, scholarly, and without ambition, David preferred the quiet realm of books and thought to the rigors of the fields or the gregarious world of the pulpit. While attending Lane University in nearby Lecompton, Kansas, David gazed up from his books long enough to catch sight of Ida Elizabeth Stover, a strong-willed, yet lovely, pacifist. The two fell in love and were married on September 23, 1885.

For some strange reason, David, who had no sense for business, opened a general store in Hope, Kansas. Three years later, with his farmer clients wallowing in the midst of a suffocating drought and unable to pay their bills, and with David spending more time studying classical literature than his accounting books, David closed the store. While Ida tended to their two sons, Arthur and Edgar, David headed to Texas to look for work, then sent for his family in 1889 after landing a job with a railroad company in Denison, Texas.

There, in a dilapidated shanty on the wrong side of the tracks, David Dwight Eisenhower was born on October 14, 1890. His mother, hating the notion that her son would be referred to as "Jr.," quickly reversed the names so that the child would be called Dwight David.

David, still uncomfortable with having to put down his books and work, failed to earn much money in Texas. When his brother-in-law offered him a job in Abilene in 1891, David, with $24.15 in his pocket, collected his family and his few meager possessions and returned to Kansas, hoping this stint would be more productive than his first.

Hope as he might, David lacked the burning intensity to ensure that his family enjoyed even a modest standard of living. For six years Ida tended to the children in another run-down structure, this one standing beside the Union Pacific railroad tracks that divided the wealthy residents of Abilene from its less fortunate citizens. Finally, in 1898 David's brother rented him a small, two-story, white frame house, an improvement for the Eisenhower family but still far from what their neighbors possessed across the tracks. The irrepressible Ida, however, made things work, and there she raised six strapping young boys (Roy, Earl, Milton, Arthur, Edgar, and Dwight—another brother, Paul, died within ten months of his birth).

The Eisenhowers never thought of themselves as poverty-stricken. Crops grown on a family farm supplemented whatever David brought home, while Ida's ingenuity and love supplied the rest. Dwight and his brothers lived a carefree life of sports, hunting, fishing, and swimming naked in a nearby pond, as if Huck Finn had been transplanted to the Kansas prairie. They fought and argued like most brothers but banded together when threatened by outsiders.

Dwight early exhibited a gift for independence. During a family reunion held on a farm shortly before his fifth birthday, Dwight encountered an ornery goose that kept charging the boy whenever he walked into the barnyard. The boy's uncle, Luther, gave him a broom handle, showed him how to swat the goose, and turned him loose. Little Dwight marched into the barnyard, stared at the offending animal, then forced it into a hasty retreat with a few well-aimed smacks with the broom. When reflecting on the incident years later, Eisenhower wrote, "This all turned out to be a rather good lesson for me because I quickly learned never to negotiate with an adversary except from a position of strength."[1]

Thus emboldened, over his childhood years the boy reenacted countless battles involving the United States cavalry and the ferocious Indians, which he inevitably won as the cavalry officer, or celebrated duels between Wild West marshals and notorious villains of the day. He read Westerns and especially adored learning about Wyatt Earp and the legendary Abilene marshal, Tom Smith. Eisenhower frequently visited Smith's grave to read the soul-stirring inscription:

> *A Fearless Hero of Frontier Days*
> *Who in Cowboy Chaos*
> *Established the Supremacy of Law.*[2]

When war flared in 1898 between the United States and Spain, Eisenhower closely followed the exploits of Admiral George Dewey, Colonel

Theodore Roosevelt, and the other heroes of that brief clash. He and his brothers took to nearby hills and rises, where they pretended to fight with Teddy Roosevelt and his Rough Riders as they annihilated the hated Spaniards.

Despite their martial spirit, the boys could not eliminate another enemy—chores. Each boy had his own to complete, such as tending the garden or chopping wood. As a reward, Dwight and Edgar could take produce grown from their own tiny gardens to the wealthier side of town, where they earned a small income selling tomatoes and corn.

The Eisenhower boys, particularly Edgar and Dwight, upheld both family honor and bragging rights against more well-to-do students in a series of bare-knuckled bouts at Garfield Junior High and Abilene High School. The pair never wearied of fighting, and they never allowed an insult from other students to go unchallenged. The two quickly earned the reputation as the best scrappers, especially after Dwight quickly dispatched the class bully. One day on the playground the student started swinging a rope with a metallic bolt attached, then dared any student to come forth and stop him. Eisenhower immediately stepped out of the throng of classmates, tackled the bully, and sent him on his way. "From that time on whenever there was any kind of trouble on the school grounds [the students] always wailed 'Ike, Ike, Ike,'"[3] said classmate John Long.

Eisenhower began attending Abilene High School in September 1904, but had to repeat the year when a life-threatening knee infection, the result of an injury from a fall from a wooden platform, caused him to miss a large portion of the school year. He returned with renewed vigor—not so much for books and knowledge as for the sporting activities he had missed. The avid football and baseball star considered school's primary importance was the opportunities it gave him to smash opponents on the football field or defeat them on the diamond.

Never one to study late into the night—or even into the early evening, for that matter—Eisenhower relied on innate ability, inquisitiveness, and intelligence to cruise through his classes. One classmate explained that he had "never heard him say, 'I don't know,'" to a teacher's query, and brother Edgar added, "His curiosity is inexhaustible. It always was."[4]

Eisenhower preferred an independent realm of thought and discussion to the classroom, where rigidly defined studies tended to bore him. He read histories and biographies whenever possible, from which he analyzed the talents and daring of men like George Washington, Hannibal, Caesar, Pericles, and Theodore Roosevelt. Instead of discussing books and ideas with a teacher, he introduced himself to Charles M. Harger, the editor of the *Abilene Daily-Reflector*. The editor discovered a bright mind in the young boy, who studiously listened to the editor's words and asked penetrating questions.

"Coming to high school age, Dwight was a natural leader," explained Harger. "He organized groups and was popular with teachers. He was no miracle child; he was just a strong, healthy boy with a serious mind, who looked upon the world as waiting for him—in what capacity he did not know."[5]

Eisenhower illustrated his natural leadership the time his football team traveled to a nearby town for a game. When the Abilene team arrived, some of the players objected to the fact that a black athlete would take the field. Eisenhower berated his teammates for their insensitivity and threatened to leave the team if they did not play. His teammates backed down, and after the game Eisenhower made a point to walk over and shake the black athlete's hand.

That Eisenhower reacted in such a manner is no surprise in light of the influences that fashioned him. Individuals from real life and from his extensive reading provided models of behavior that the young Eisenhower absorbed. The qualities for which he admired certain people as a schoolchild would later appear in his own handling of situations and headstrong associates.

Two of the historic figures he hoped to emulate offered lessons in determination, single-mindedness, and patience. He praised George Washington's absolute belief in his cause and in his actions during the American Revolution, even though the odds had offered convincing reasons why he might be wrong and confidants had suggested alternative courses. As he wrote in his memoirs, Eisenhower admired Washington because of his "stamina and patience in adversity, first, and then his indomitable courage, daring, and capacity for self-sacrifice."

At the same time, Eisenhower never forgot the story of General George G. Meade at Gettysburg. On July 2, 1863, with the critical phase of the famous Civil War clash staring him in the face, General Meade rode about the terrain, alone with his thoughts and doubts, formulating the plans for his encounter with Robert E. Lee. "For Meade," Eisenhower later wrote in his memoirs, "this was the moment of truth when all within him, particularly his moral courage, had to bear tough and strong on the problem ahead. No council of war could be called. No delay for leisurely study would be permitted by Lee. The decision had to be made. And the decision was solely Meade's responsibility."

Once Meade had decided on a course of action, he quietly rode toward his aides, issued his orders, then waited for the battle to commence. Meade's calm assurance in the propriety of his course of action, done without histrionics or drama, impressed Eisenhower, for Meade faced that decision with "only the loneliness of one man on whose mind weighed the fate of ninety thousand comrades and of the Republic they served. Meade's claim to greatness in that moment may very well be best evidenced by the total absence of the theatrical."[6]

Three Abilene residents influenced Eisenhower as well. Every town resident knew Bob Davis, a man who typified the city's Wild West heritage. He taught Eisenhower how to fish, hunt, shoot a gun, and adapt to the rigorous outdoor environment of the Kansas plains. More importantly, he imparted the ability to quickly evaluate people and situations and react accordingly. Eisenhower's legendary skill at poker, for instance, in which he studied both the cards already played and his opponents' habits, was taught to him by Davis as they sat around a campfire at night.

In addition to Charles M. Harger, Joseph Howe, a local businessman who had traveled extensively and owned a huge library of great literature, opened a world beyond Abilene for the high school student. While some of his classmates were content to grow up and live within a thirty-mile radius of Abilene, Eisenhower yearned to see more of the world. "I like to read what's going on outside of Kansas," he told Howe. "Makes me realize that Kansas isn't the whole world."[7] Harger and Howe strengthened Eisenhower's belief that the way things were done in Kansas or the United States did not necessarily mean that other systems were wrong.

When it came to parental influence, one person dominated. Eisenhower's sullen, withdrawn father rarely played a role in his son's life, mainly because he usually was not present. David Eisenhower left early for work, came home for dinner, and then immediately retreated to his room and books. The only time the sons interacted with their father was when one needed to be disciplined.

Ida more than made up for her husband's shortcomings. "Mother was by far the greatest personal influence in our lives,"[8] Eisenhower stated years later. She imparted discipline with fairness. For instance, to avoid partiality she set up the weekly chores, such as feeding the chickens or milking the cows, on a rotating basis. Each boy not only learned how to perform the task, but also knew he would soon be relieved of any he considered distasteful. If two boys argued over how to divide a cake, she told one to cut the cake and allowed the other to select first.

The mother, a firm pacifist and reader of the Bible, delivered a stream of aphorisms as guidance to her growing sons. She had a list ready whenever one or more were faced with a difficult situation; the boys just did not know which of her favorites she might employ. "The Lord deals the cards, and you play them," or "Sink or swim. Survive or perish" vied with "Nothing comes easy in life."[9] Ida wanted her boys to be independent instead of looking to their parents for salvation. She explained that a person should do what was right, not from fear of punishment but because it was the right thing to do. She encouraged them to develop dreams and told them that they could accomplish anything if they were willing to work and sacrifice. Above all, she wanted her boys to accept their successes with humility and to realize that a poverty-stricken individual has as much worth as a king.

Lessons came even with punishment. When his parents told the ten-year-old Eisenhower he could not go out with his older brothers on Halloween, Eisenhower rushed outside and pounded a tree until his fists bled. After his father punished him for his tantrum, Ida walked in, sat on his bed, and told Eisenhower that he would never succeed until he controlled that fiery temper. "He that conquereth his own soul is greater than he who taketh a city," she admonished her son. She added that anger and hatred hurt only the person grappling with those emotions, not anyone or anything they might be directed against. "I have always looked back on that conversation as one of the most valuable moments of my life,"[10] Eisenhower wrote after serving as president.

He also learned a lesson in diplomacy by watching his mother. One time Ida mentioned to her husband that he had to fix a broken window shade. The sullen man replied he did not have to do anything and headed for his room. A few days later Ida walked up to David and said, "Dave, I wonder if you could do this: I can't seem to get it done."[11] With that less-threatening tack, David repaired the shade.

+=—=+

On May 27, 1909, Eisenhower graduated from high school. According to the school prediction, he was headed to Yale as a history professor, but he and brother Edgar made their own plans. Lacking money for both of them to attend college simultaneously, Dwight remained in Abilene and worked for a year while Edgar enrolled in law at the University of Michigan. They intended to reverse roles each year until, after eight years, both had graduated. Eisenhower shared one goal with each of his five brothers—he wanted to leave Abilene and avoid being trapped in his father's world.

Close friend Everett E. "Swede" Hazlett Jr. offered a possible remedy. Hazlett, who had received an appointment to the United States Naval Academy at Annapolis, urged Eisenhower to seek his own appointment so they could attend together. Eisenhower felt he had nothing to lose by following Hazlett's advice, and on August 20, 1910, he sent a letter to Senator Joseph L. Bristow. "I would very much like to enter either the school at Annapolis, or the one at West Point. In order to do this, I must have an appointment to one of these places and so I am writing to you in order to secure the same."[12]

When he learned that at age 21 he would be too old for Annapolis, Eisenhower pinned his hopes on West Point. He placed second in the qualifying examinations, but became Bristow's choice when the top-ranked candidate failed the physical exams. Thus, accepted as an alternate candidate, Eisenhower received orders to report to West Point on June 14, 1911. Eisenhower beamed at the prospect of attending a renowned institution at taxpayer's expense and of playing football for West Point.

After saying goodbye to family and friends, Eisenhower boarded the train that would take him from Kansas to New York. He first stopped in Ann Arbor, Michigan, to visit his brother Edgar and had such a pleasant time—the college girls particularly interested him—he wondered if he should have applied to the University of Michigan instead. However, the lure of a free education overcame any doubts.

Eisenhower's first day at West Point tested his physical and mental capabilities. It seemed that wherever he turned, upperclassmen materialized with fresh orders—all shouted at the tops of their lungs. Eisenhower loved the strict regimen, however. Later that evening, when he and the other incoming students were sworn in as cadets of the academy, with the flag snapping in the breeze nearby, an impressed Eisenhower realized for the first time he was at the service of his country.

The mood did not last long. For Eisenhower, who had never enjoyed the stultifying regimen imposed by schools, West Point's classrooms were torture. Teachers were usually former graduates who taught the identical curriculum they studied, in the same fashion they had learned—memorization. Creativity and independent thought had little place in the rigid structure in which teachers wanted the "accepted" West Point answer to a military problem and expected the students to list in order the battalions and regiments serving under Ulysses S. Grant. Eisenhower studied enough to receive decent grades but refused to put much time into something he considered unnecessary when football offered more excitement.

Consequently, Eisenhower compiled a large number of demerits, usually for minor infractions such as being late for breakfast or for smoking in his room. He simply did not care about matters he considered trivial—and these things shrank in comparison to playing football and obtaining an education for free. Eisenhower had not selected West Point from a burning desire to command armies and defeat enemies. He was there because it was free and because he hoped to star on the football field.

Eisenhower enjoyed his experience at West Point, where he not only met fascinating individuals from all corners of the nation but could envision a future in which he could see the world. Years later, as Eisenhower lay on his deathbed after decades of fame as a general and as a president, the sole portion of his life he wanted to talk about was his time at West Point—not his leadership that defeated Hitler, not his decisions in the weary hours before the D-Day assault, not his feats as president.

In one way, at least, it was odd that Eisenhower so fondly recalled those days, for he did not acquire his military education until later, when he worked for outstanding officers. His West Point classroom teachers made little impression on him, and most of the learning he acquired came about either accidentally or through personal observation and experience.

During the summer of 1912, for instance, a plebe (first-year student) accidentally bumped into Eisenhower, who was now an upperclassman. An irritated Eisenhower tore into the hapless plebe, then barked that he looked like he had done nothing more before coming to West Point than being a lowly barber. When the plebe answered that he had, in fact, been a barber, an embarrassed Eisenhower quickly ended the encounter. Feeling remorse that he had mocked the occupation of another individual, Eisenhower told his roommate, "I've just done something that was stupid and unforgivable. I managed to make a man ashamed of the work he did for a living."[13] He vowed to never again so humiliate a person.

Eisenhower had few such problems on the football field, one arena in which he did not embarrass himself. He frequently remained so late on the field practicing punts that he missed the rubbing table, and the team trainer complained that Eisenhower kept him retrieving footballs until well after dark.

Eisenhower's hard-nosed style of play endeared him to coaches and intimidated opponents. For the rest of his life, Eisenhower relished the memory of when he and a teammate so viciously smacked the legendary athlete Jim Thorpe that Thorpe had to leave the game. On the other hand, he also recalled watching the 1913 game against Notre Dame, when the duo of Gus Dorais and Knute Rockne first brought the forward pass to the nation's attention in a stunning 35–13 upset over Army.

Eisenhower placed so much importance on sports, particularly football, that he often judged a person in a positive manner if that individual played sports. No other endeavor that he had experienced placed such emphasis on teamwork and the development of leadership. "I believe that football, perhaps more than any other sport, tends to instill in men the feeling that victory comes through hard—almost slavish—work, team play, self-confidence, and an enthusiasm that amounts to dedication."[14] Throughout his career, Eisenhower looked for those abilities in the men he chose to command for him.

Eisenhower's football career ended in the fall of 1912 when he badly twisted his knee trying to gain a few additional yards in a game against Tufts. When he further aggravated it shortly afterward in a riding drill, Eisenhower had to abandon his prime love. He so badly sulked about West Point that others started calling him "Gloomy Face," and Eisenhower even considered leaving the academy. However, his mood eventually improved and Eisenhower turned to less physical sports. At least, he mused, he would obtain a college education.

Shortly before graduation in 1915 Eisenhower learned that, because of his football injury, the army was questioning whether to offer him a commission in the service. The academy surgeon, Lieutenant Colonel Henry A. Shaw, agreed to recommend Eisenhower if the young man applied for the coast artillery, a sedate posting that offered little hope of action or advancement. Eisenhower rejected the offer and started examining other possibilities, including that of being an Argentine cowboy. A few days later Shaw returned with a modified offer: If Eisenhower promised not to apply for the cavalry, Shaw would recommend him fit for service. Eisenhower concurred and applied for a posting with the infantry.

On June 12, 1915, Eisenhower graduated and received a commission as a second lieutenant. He was a proud part of what was later labeled the "class the stars fell on" because so many went on to become generals in World War II, including Omar N. Bradley. While everyone assumed Bradley would attain success, few recognized similar talent in Eisenhower. One West Point officer concluded, "We did not see in him a man who would throw himself into his job so completely that nothing else would matter."[15]

Based on Eisenhower's record, this was a fair assessment. He attended West Point for the opportunity to play football and because the education was free, not because he yearned to be a general or cherished dreams of serving his country. Having amassed more demerits than accolades in his four years, Eisenhower finished a mediocre 61st academically out of 164 class members. He also ranked 125th in discipline.

Nonetheless, he had his degree and commission, and now the young man from Kansas would see where it took him. He held few illusions. At this point the military had been a means of attaining something else, not a lifelong dream. His outlook would change as he faced a succession of challenges and, especially, as he met a series of mentors. Eisenhower's classroom would prove to be in the field.

PART II

Education of an Officer

CHAPTER 2

"I Want to Go Overseas"

AFTER GRADUATION EISENHOWER RETURNED TO ABILENE FOR A brief vacation while waiting for his first assignment. He spent most of his time with Gladys Harding, a high school classmate for whom he had developed such deep feelings that he eventually asked her to marry him. Harding declined because she wanted to pursue a musical career and because her father scoffed at the notion that Eisenhower would ever amount to anything. A disappointed Eisenhower turned his attention to other matters.

Drawn by the lure of duty in the distant Far East, Eisenhower hoped to be sent to the Philippines, but border incidents along the Texas-Mexico boundary determined his first assignment. In September 1915 he reported to Fort Sam Houston near San Antonio, Texas, to begin his life with the military as a second lieutenant in the 19th Infantry Regiment.

Life in the Regular Army in those pre–World War I days was hardly enticing. Fewer than 5,000 officers supervised a little over 100,000 enlisted men, meaning that the nation could barely mount more than a minor operation against second-rate foes. Low pay and harsh conditions guaranteed that the service attracted a rougher element, with drunkenness and high desertion rates as the result. Officers had to rely on strict discipline to bring order to what could easily become a chaotic situation.

With a new career unfolding before him, Eisenhower decided to put more effort into his work than he had given at West Point. He had not yet developed a burning desire to excel—which had been reserved for sports—but Eisenhower concluded if he was to be in the service, he may as well make the most of it.

Eisenhower did not enjoy a smooth beginning in the field. One of his earliest duties was as provost marshal, the officer in charge of maintaining order. The task offered few challenges when dealing with situations at Fort Sam Houston itself, but Eisenhower faced new problems when the soldiers headed to town, where San Antonio's numerous bars and prostitutes created situations ready-made for brawls. "We had a certain amount of trouble keeping order for a while, with untrained soldiers and time on their hands . . ."[1] recalled Eisenhower of his military initiation. He solved the quandary by personally patrolling the town's streets with his men.

While Eisenhower struggled with his adjustment to the world of supervision, he succeeded in the world of love. In October 1915 one of Eisenhower's friends, Leonard Gerow, introduced him to Mamie Geneva Doud. He was so captivated by the young woman that in the days immediately following the introduction, despite the fact that she had dates with other men, Eisenhower would wait at her doorstep. If Mamie was not there, he sat on the porch, visiting with her father, until the girl returned, determined to impress Mamie and to show his competition he meant business. Eisenhower's efforts were in vain until Mamie's father, who enjoyed the officer's presence and resolve and knew his daughter was just playing hard to get, finally told her, "Stop this flighty nonsense, or the Army boy will give up in disgust."[2] Mamie finally accepted a date.

Eisenhower never formally asked Mamie to marry him. On Valentine's Day 1916, he simply handed her a replica of his West Point class ring, which was the custom for a graduate intending to marry.

Eisenhower, attracted by the excitement offered by flying and by a fifty percent pay increase, had applied for duty with the service's fledgling aviation arm. Mamie's father, shocked at the appalling death rate among pilots, protested that he was not about to allow his daughter to become a widow so soon in her life. Eisenhower chose romance over adventure and agreed to rescind his application. Mamie and he were married on July 1, 1916, the same day that Eisenhower learned he had been promoted to first lieutenant.

As was the case throughout their married life, the Eisenhowers opened their home on base to friends and their spouses. "Club Eisenhower" became a mainstay for a tight group of young officers, where they shared stories, compared experiences, discussed military theory, and played cards. Not only was it a way to learn from one another, but for the financially strapped officers, it was a relatively inexpensive form of entertainment. Had Mamie's father not sent $100 a month support for much of their early married life, the Eisenhowers might not have made it though the first difficult years.

The biggest excitement at Fort Sam Houston came from south of the border, where an ongoing series of disturbances threatened the peace. When the Mexican outlaw and political leader Pancho Villa raided Columbus, New Mexico in March 1916, killing eighteen American citizens, President Woodrow Wilson dispatched a punitive expedition under Brigadier General John J. Pershing to hunt down the offender. Eager for a chance at combat, Eisenhower asked for an immediate transfer to Pershing's command, but as was often the case throughout his career, superiors denied the request. They had an abundance of such appeals and could not assent to all. Instead, Eisenhower received orders temporarily assigning him to Camp Wilson near Austin, Texas, to train an Illinois National Guard unit consisting mainly of Chicago-area Irish. A dejected Mamie wondered how her new husband could leave her so soon after their wedding. She could not have been reassured to hear Eisenhower's response, but the young officer, now faced with the responsibilities of command, had become more serious in his approach to his occupation. "There's one thing you must understand," he told his spouse, "My country comes first and always will. You come second."[3]

Despite his disappointment at being left out of the fighting, Eisenhower masked his feelings and gave full effort to his training assignment. He insisted on respect from his men, arduous training exercises, attention to detail, and fairness, all which endeared him to the men he commanded. He also used his disappointment as a prod—if he could not be in the field with Pershing, he was going to make certain he did not miss out on the next opportunity. For the first time in his career, Eisenhower started to take his job seriously. "As I look back on it, it [1916] was one of the valuable years of preparation in my early career," Eisenhower wrote later. "I began to devote more hours of study and reading to my profession . . ."[4] He was certain that one day, as long as he applied himself, he would see combat duty.

He thought his chance had arrived in April 1917 when President Wilson, angered by the loss of American lives at the hands of German submarines, asked Congress to declare war. Eisenhower requested a transfer to a unit headed overseas, but once again superiors, impressed with his training of the national guard unit, felt he would be more valuable in a stateside post. Instead of joining most of his classmates on the battlefields of France, commanding troops and furthering his military career, Eisenhower helped assemble a new regiment being formed in Texas. Somewhat mollified by a May promotion to captain, Eisenhower focused on his responsibilities and hoped that would gain him access to the front.

In September he was transferred to Fort Oglethorpe in Georgia to train officers headed for Europe. Never having been under fire, and possessing little knowledge of combat situations in the mud and slime of France, Eisenhower scoured newspapers for information that would help him prepare the officers for what they were about to experience. He designed and constructed an elaborate mock battlefield at Fort Oglethorpe, complete with dugouts, trenches, and barbed wire, and put the officers through as realistic a course of instruction as possible. Eisenhower knew he could only deliver a semblance of reality, but he intended to be as accurate as he possibly could so far from the front.

The birth of his first son, Doud Dwight Eisenhower, on September 24, 1917, eased his anguish at being left out of the fighting. Nicknamed

Icky, the boy breathed the pride and satisfaction into the young officer that he failed to receive from his duties.

The army closed Fort Oglethorpe in December 1917 and ordered Eisenhower to Fort Leavenworth, Kansas, to train at the Army Service School. Again irritated at being denied a chance to cross the Atlantic and fight the Germans, Eisenhower submitted yet another request to be sent overseas. When Leavenworth's commandant called him into his office and berated the young officer for not following orders, a chagrined Eisenhower challenged his superior to explain when it became wrong for an officer to seek combat. At a loss for an explanation, the commandant complimented Eisenhower for his willingness to stand up for himself but could do nothing to alter the situation. Eisenhower was stuck in the distant plains of Kansas while West Point classmates gained valuable combat experience. The incident reinforced Eisenhower's anger toward a staff officer somewhere in Washington, D.C., who routinely declined his requests for the front. "A man at a desk a thousand miles away knew better than I what my military capabilities and talents were . . ."[5] he wrote sarcastically years later. He would forever be suspicious of staff officers who wielded inordinate power over others.

Like a dutiful soldier, however, Eisenhower swallowed his emotions and applied himself to his new duties. If he was going to be in Kansas to train soldiers, then he intended to make them the best trained men in the Army. He put the men through rigorous training exercises, demanded perfection in every detail, and executed every drill with enthusiasm and excitement. Sensing that the men detested the routine bayonet drills, Eisenhower brought a bit of college football to the endeavor by cheering his men on, as if they were halfbacks and quarterbacks. One soldier later wrote home, "Our new Captain, Eisenhower by name, is, I believe, one of the most efficient and best Army officers in the country . . . He has given us wonderful bayonet drills. He gets the fellows' imaginations worked up and hollers and yells and makes us shout and stomp until we go tearing into the air as if we meant business."[6]

Eisenhower was not only well loved by the enlisted men. One of his lieutenants preferred Eisenhower's unique style of training to the stilted efforts of previous men. Eisenhower's enthusiasm and apparent knowledge of battlefield conditions convinced every man that what they learned under Eisenhower would later help them in combat. The lieutenant wrote that Eisenhower "is a corker and has put more fight into us in three days than we got in all the previous time we were here."[7]

The enlisted men also respected Eisenhower because he treated them fairly. They sometimes cursed the officer's rigorous training schedule and his insistence that everything be done properly, but they knew he had their best interests at heart. One time Eisenhower noticed one of his officers chewing out an enlisted man in front of his unit. Recalling the time when he embarrassed the plebe at West Point, Eisenhower called the lieutenant into his office to discuss the matter. He told the young man that an officer could never create a cohesive unit through embarrassment. Instead, he had to rely on fairness, proper treatment, and leadership through example.

He made a large impression in a short time, and two months after arriving at Fort Leavenworth, Eisenhower received orders to report to Camp Meade, Maryland, where he would train men to use one of the army's newest weapons—the tank. Lieutenant Colonel Ira Welborn, a Medal of Honor winner, had observed Eisenhower's expertise in training in Georgia. When the army searched for a talented officer to oversee early training with the tank, a weapon many considered important for breaking the stalemate that mired Europe in trench warfare, Welborn recommended the young captain.

For once, Eisenhower eagerly greeted the news, for he assumed that in training a tank outfit, he would naturally accompany it when it went overseas. In addition, the tank was so innovative that he would be breaking new ground in almost anything he accomplished, a fact that was certain to draw notice. At last, he thought, that distant French battlefield drew closer.

Eisenhower prepared more diligently with the 301st Tank Battalion than with his prior assignments, as he expected that his work would be continued in France. His efforts appeared to be rewarded when in March 1918 he learned that the unit was earmarked for overseas duty.

Once again, however, Eisenhower's hopes evaporated when the army sent him to Camp Colt near Gettysburg for more training. Eisenhower became a victim of a vicious circle: Disappointed over the lack of combat, he worked more assiduously in his training to enhance his chances for overseas duty, but the better he performed in training, the more the army wanted to retain him in the United States.

"Some of my class were already in France. Others were ready to depart. I seemed embedded in the monotony and unsought safety of the Zone of the Interior," he wrote in his memoirs. Eisenhower saw his military career tumbling down into an endless string of staff and training assignments while his classmates found glory on the battlefield. "It looked to me as if anyone who was denied the opportunity to fight might as well get out of the Army at the end of the war."[8]

Again, Eisenhower dutifully set aside his frustrations and, with few resources at his disposal, commenced assembling what became the largest tank-training center in the country. Lacking even a single tank for training purposes—the few that existed rumbled across French terrain—Eisenhower collected any vehicles he could find, bolted machine guns to them, then headed to Gettysburg's surrounding countryside to practice maneuvers. One of his drills required gunners to fire at famed Little Round Top, the scene of memorable fighting during the 1863 Battle of Gettysburg, as their truck bounced along rough roads. Eisenhower knew he could not simulate actual combat, but he figured this would give his gunners an idea of what conditions might be like once they landed in Europe.

His time in training troops at least allowed Eisenhower to begin formulating his method of command. He insisted on rigorous discipline, but he also conveyed such an interest in his men that they knew they could enter his office to discuss military or personal problems. He refused to surround himself with compliant officers who eagerly carried out his every wish without question. When one lieutenant told Eisenhower he saw nothing wrong with conditions at the camp, Eisenhower prodded him to examine things more closely by saying, "I want you to figure out some things which are wrong with this camp. You make me uncomfortable by always agreeing with me . . . you either don't say what you think, or you are as big a fool as I am!"[9]

When firm action was needed, Eisenhower never wavered. Eisenhower had banned alcohol for his men. One hotel owner in town, though agreeing to the ban, continued to serve alcohol to Eisenhower's men. When Eisenhower placed a guard at the hotel to prevent his men from entering, a move that cut into the owner's profits, the man stormed into Eisenhower's office with his congressman in tow. The politician, figuring the young officer would quickly crumble, threatened to go to the War Department unless Eisenhower removed the guard.

"You do just exactly that," Eisenhower shot back. "Nothing would please me better than to be taken out of this job. I want to go overseas. If they take me out of here, maybe I can get there."[10]

The pair hustled from Eisenhower's office, threatening to ruin his career, but the War Department saw through the ploy. The assistant secretary of war even sent Eisenhower a flattering letter in which he praised the young man for his handling of the event.

That was not the only confrontation Eisenhower faced with a congressman at Camp Colt. When Eisenhower learned that a young officer had used a marked deck in playing poker, Eisenhower told him to make a choice—either resign or face a court-martial. The officer resigned but returned a few days later with his father and his congressman. The trio attempted to persuade Eisenhower to soften the penalty, but Eisenhower believed that without honesty, an officer lost his effectiveness. He refused to change his decision and explained that if he transferred the man to a new post, as they requested, he would only be handing off the problem to a fellow officer. Through the congressman's influence, the officer eventually gained a post in a different unit, but Eisenhower had held his ground. The man was no longer serving in his command.

Eisenhower's sergeant major, Claude J. Harris, had the chance to observe his commanding officer during these months at Camp Colt. Harris's unique perspective—working closely with officers, yet reared an enlisted man—provides a valuable summation of Eisenhower's strong points. According to Eisenhower biographer Stephen Ambrose, Harris said that, "Eisenhower was a strict disciplinarian, an inborn soldier, but most human, considerate. . . . Despite his youth, he possessed a high understanding of organization, the ability to place an estimate on a man and fit him into a position where he would 'click.'" Harris added that Eisenhower's command style "built for him high admiration and loyalty from his officers perhaps unequaled by few commanding officers."[11]

Within seven months, Eisenhower commanded 10,000 men and 600 officers. He performed so well that he received a promotion to lieutenant colonel.

Eisenhower thought he had been doubly rewarded when Colonel Welborn informed him that he was going to be sent overseas with the tank regiment he trained. The United States planned an immense 1919 spring offensive in which tanks were to play a prominent role.

An excited Eisenhower prepared to finally join his West Point classmates along the front lines of Europe. Once again, however, the goal eluded his grasp with the war's termination in November 1918. Eisenhower was chatting with a fellow officer, Captain Norman Randolph, when the news arrived. He had missed his chance at a war.

Despite laboring thousands of miles from the front, Eisenhower honed valuable skills during the war years. He had shown an ability to organize and lead men, he saw the value of thorough training, and he had gained priceless experience dealing with politicians and civilians. One of his superiors commended him for showing that, though he was only three years out of West Point, he could execute the responsibilities in commands often held by brigadier generals.

Eisenhower received the Distinguished Service Medal as a result of his contributions, but the medal meant little to the career officer. He had missed his chance at combat, and who knew when another opportunity might arise. However, he swallowed his anguish and decided to work his way out of the frustrating situation. With iron determination, Eisenhower stated to Randolph after learning of the war's end, "By God! From now on I'm cutting myself a swath that will make up for this!"[12]

CHAPTER 3

"An Incalculable Debt"

THE 1920S AND 1930S PROVED TO BE DECADES OF EXCELLENT preparation for Eisenhower. While other officers pondered whether to leave the peacetime army, the Kansan settled in to a series of assignments that helped him fashion the command style that he would employ in World War II. Rather than learning his trade in the classroom—which had always bored him—Eisenhower absorbed lessons in leadership through action in the field and through association with gifted commanders such as Fox Conner. In these years he also forged a series of alliances with influential men who shaped his career.

Still disappointed that he had missed the fighting in Europe, in 1919 Eisenhower volunteered to be part of a transcontinental motor expedition that would test the military's capabilities at moving across the United States, show the necessity for improved roads, and gain publicity for an army that was quickly being forgotten in peacetime America. In conjunction with automobile and tire companies, the War Department planned to send 72 vehicles and 280 officers and enlisted men from Washington, D.C., to San Francisco, largely following the route that Interstate 80 would one day provide.

The caravan departed on July 7, 1919. As expected, it experienced a wide range of roads, from sporadically paved thoroughfares that permitted swift access to numerous dirt and mud paths that slowed movement to a few miles per hour. In its 62 days, the expedition averaged 58 miles a day at a speed of 6 miles per hour, and visited a collection of towns that staged parades and welcoming banquets for the men.

Eisenhower considered the journey a vacation. He and a fellow officer, Major Sereno Brett, loved to pull practical jokes on the civilians who accompanied the group, such as tricking them in Wyoming into thinking that hostile Indians were about to attack. In all, the trip was a welcome distraction from his anguish over being retained in the United States during the war.

Despite the levity of his own behavior, Eisenhower thought the commanding officer was too lax with his men. In a subsequent report, he wrote that the officer failed to insist on proper discipline and that he did not schedule regular drills and exercises to keep the men sharp. In addition, Eisenhower learned much about the sorry state of American roads, which he believed had to be upgraded for both vacationers yearning to visit different parts of the country as well as for the military intending to defend it. Eisenhower rarely participated in any military activity without learning something or without taking the matter seriously.

The condition of the military in postwar America mirrored the sorry state of the nation's road system. Weary of conflict and deaths, especially those raging in faraway Europe, Americans wanted nothing but calm and peace. Consequently, in the 1920s the World War I machine quickly disintegrated to a core of dedicated officers, like Eisenhower, commanding an army that numerically lagged behind most major nations. In 1922 Congress set a limit of 12,000 commissioned officers and 125,000 enlisted men for the Army, a figure that did not rise until the mid-1930s and consigned the army to a ranking of seventeenth among world nations.

Eisenhower did not escape the turbulent times, either personally or professionally. One of the happiest moments of his life had been the birth of his son, Doud Dwight, in 1917. Eisenhower adored the boy, nicknamed Icky. The child loved spending time with the soldiers under Eisenhower's command, who purchased a uniform for Icky and, with permission, took him out on minor drills. A proud father boasted that Icky "was just one of the boys."[1]

But the idyll did not last. During Christmas 1920, doctors diagnosed Icky with scarlet fever and Eisenhower's world collapsed. Physicians warned Eisenhower that either the then-untreatable disease would gradually fade, which would leave Icky weakened but well, or it would worsen and Icky could die. As he later wrote in his memoirs, a distraught Eisenhower "haunted the halls of the hospital" hoping to convey some form of mental strength to his young child. The illness turned into meningitis, and on January 2, 1921, with his small red bicycle still resting under the Christmas tree, Icky succumbed to the disease.

"This was the greatest disappointment and disaster in my life, the one I have never been able to forget completely," Eisenhower wrote in 1967, the first time he publicly mentioned the painful ordeal. "Today when I think of it, even now as I write of it, the keenness of our loss comes back to me as fresh and terrible as it was in that long dark day soon after Christmas, 1920."[2]

At such an agonizing time, husband and wife turned inward rather than toward each other to deal with their own grief. Both kept their feelings, emotions, and words deeply concealed, and Eisenhower later confided in his memoirs that, "I didn't know what to do. I blamed myself . . ." for his death. However, every year following Icky's death, Eisenhower sent yellow roses to Mamie on Icky's birthday—yellow had been the little boy's favorite color.

The death rattled a normally imperturbable Eisenhower. Some friends claimed that he became more distant from people following the episode. Others stated that he applied all his energies to his career, seeking comfort in his military duties that he could find nowhere else.

His miseries continued. The army rejected his application to infantry school at Fort Benning, Georgia, a crucial step for those wishing to advance. A rough summer followed Icky's death. Before Icky's illness Eisenhower had accepted from the army $250 earmarked for dependent support at a time when the child was with his mother in Iowa. Eisenhower had no idea that taking the money while his son was living with his mother might be wrong as other officers had done the same, and his arguments allowed investigators to conclude no punishable crime had been committed and thus no official court-martial was necessary. A court-martial could have ended Eisenhower's career, and the fact that he had been exonerated mattered little. The affair so bothered him that he never again referred to it.

Eisenhower saw this frustrating period as a dead end to his military life and wondered if he should leave the military and seek employment in the public sector. Many of his fellow officers had taken lucrative posts in civilian professions and urged him to do the same, but ultimately he declined. He loved his profession, a point Mamie emphasized in discussing the future. "Well, Ike, I don't think you'd be happy [if you leave]. This is your life and you know it and you like it."[3] Eisenhower listened to his wife's wisdom and did not resign.

The birth of another son, John, in 1922 eased Eisenhower's pain over Icky's death, as did his association with George Patton and Fox Conner, powerful intellectual men. They challenged Eisenhower's outlook on the role of the military, prepared him for higher command, and helped shape his military personality. Eisenhower took valuable lessons from each.

In September 1919, after completing the transcontinental motor expedition, Eisenhower returned to Camp Meade, Maryland, to become a part of the small postwar Tank Corps. He quickly bonded with another promising officer, George Patton, who like Eisenhower believed that the tank would play a prominent role in any future war. The two started what became a lifelong friendship. They spent days debating the proper use of the tank and experimenting in the field with the lumbering machines.

Their ambition to understand the machine in its smallest detail was such that they even dismantled one tank, then laboriously reassembled and drove it.

Their love for the tank placed them at odds with army doctrine, which declared that the prime use of a tank in battle was to support the infantry and crash through no man's land. Thus, according to doctrine, the tank needed to move at no higher speed than three miles per hour, the normal rate of an infantry advance. Patton and Eisenhower contended that the tank should rush ahead of the infantry at high speed, crash through or envelop the enemy, then create chaos while the infantry followed. To them, the tank was an offensive weapon on its own, not merely a supporting device.

"The clumsy, awkward and snail-like progress of the old tanks must be forgotten, and in their place we must picture this speedy, reliable and efficient engine of destruction," Eisenhower advocated in a November 1920 article that appeared in *Infantry Journal.* He knew he faced an uphill battle, for he admitted in the same piece that, "a great many officers are prone to denounce the tanks as a freak development of trench warfare which has already outlived its usefulness. Others, and this class seems to be in the majority, have come into contact with the tank so infrequently, and have heard so little either decidedly for or against it, that they simply ignore it in their calculations and mental pictures of future battles."[4]

Eisenhower blossomed during this period, as he found a kindred soul in the impetuous, self-confident Patton. The two spent hours tinkering with tanks and arguing their case for the tank's inclusion as an offensive arm of its own. "George and I had the enthusiasm of zealots,"[5] he later wrote, and reinforced with such fervor, the pair promoted the tank at every opportunity. As he had shown in his avid pursuit of Mamie, Eisenhower brought a single-minded devotion to a cause in which he believed. Once convinced, he could not easily be deterred from reaching his goal.

Patton declared that in the next war—which he and Eisenhower both believed would inevitably occur as a result of the harsh terms of the Versailles Peace Treaty forced on Germany to end World War I—that they could revive a modern-day version of a successful Civil War duo. "I'll be [Stonewall] Jackson, you'll be [Robert E.] Lee. I don't want to do the heavy thinking," Patton told his friend, "you do that and I'll get loose among our #&*?!&%* [sic] enemies."[6]

Eisenhower and Patton stood twenty years ahead of their Army colleagues in developing tank doctrine. A few military theorists, most notably J. F. C. Fuller and B. H. Liddell Hart, had promoted similar notions in England, but the ideas had yet to circulate in the United States. As far as Eisenhower and Patton knew, they were breaking original ground.

As is the case with most zealots, however, Eisenhower butted heads with superiors who contended that the weapons and the methods of employing them that succeeded in World War I would triumph again in the future. The army wanted weapons that helped infantry cross no man's land, not weapons that operated on their own. Eisenhower's advocacy of the tank so angered the chief of infantry, Major General Charles S. Farnsworth, that in the autumn of 1920 he summoned Eisenhower to his office and cautioned the young man that if he persisted in his campaign, he faced a court-martial. When Patton received a similar rebuke from Farnsworth, the pair eased back, but the rebuttals only drew them closer together.

Oddly, however, as Eisenhower's work with the tank at Fort Meade incurred the ire of his superiors, in 1919 it also brought him into contact with the man who would most influence his career. Brigadier General Fox Conner, one of the most brilliant minds in the army, asked to tour Camp Meade with Eisenhower and Patton so he could observe their work. As the trio walked about the grounds, Conner asked complex questions that these two younger officers handled with ease. Eisenhower, more accustomed to perfunctory visits by higher-ranking officers, was impressed with Conner's interest in what he and Patton were doing.

A short time later, Fox Conner contacted Eisenhower and asked him to come to Panama with him as his executive officer. The offer delighted Eisenhower, who saw this as an opportunity to advance his career now that the tank had been nudged aside by Farnsworth. In December 1921 Eisenhower was ordered to Panama.

Eisenhower and his wife boarded a troop transport in early 1922 for the voyage to Panama. As commander of the troops aboard the ship, Eisenhower enjoyed fine accommodations, but he and Mamie had to switch to cramped confines when two generals insisted that they be provided more luxurious quarters, even though, unlike Eisenhower, they had no official duties. Eisenhower chafed at this blatant misuse of authority and vowed never to behave in this manner himself.

The only things worse than their new quarters aboard ship were the living conditions they would soon have in Panama. He and Mamie lived in a squalid home—little more than a shack, really—that leaked whenever it rained and housed a group of bats that frightened Mamie. Unlike most army posts, little entertainment existed to lighten their predicament—a Wednesday night bridge club and a Friday dance served as their only outlets. The miserable conditions placed an added strain on their marriage, as Mamie had few opportunities to relieve the boredom and oppressive heat.

Eisenhower at least had military matters to take his mind off the gloom. Swede Hazlett, the close friend from Abilene who had attended the Naval Academy in Annapolis, stopped by when the submarine on which he served came through the Canal Zone, giving Eisenhower the chance to tour the boat. As Hazlett recalled, the submarine captivated his friend. "Whenever I was otherwise engaged he wandered through the ship, chatting informally with the crew—and they responded readily. I really believe that by the time he left the ship he knew almost as much about submarines as I did."[7] Eisenhower's inquisitiveness and friendliness with the enlisted men impressed Hazlett and the crew.

Despite the hardships, the weather, and duty at a far-flung outpost, Eisenhower later concluded that, "*my* [italics his] tour of duty was one of the most interesting and constructive of my life. The main reason was the presence of one man—General Fox Conner."[8]

Conner spent hours talking to Eisenhower about the attributes of command, military tactics and strategy, and the lessons taught by history. Unlike the memorization insisted upon at West Point, which Eisenhower had detested, this method of learning was like a tour through past military campaigns with Conner as a guide, breathing life and clarity into what had formerly been dull. Conner freely handed over volumes from his ample library for Eisenhower to read, then asked for his thoughts about various characters and decisions, and what he would do differently had he been in their place. He asked Eisenhower to read historical novels of different periods to gain a flavor for the times, then directed him to memoirs and biographies of important individuals.

Frequently, the discussions occurred as the two rode through the Panamanian jungles, inspecting the troops that defended the canal. When they were finished for the day, Conner and Eisenhower sat about a campfire and debated into the night. Shakespeare, Plato, Clausewitz—all became fodder for the men to digest and analyze together. No matter the subject of their conversation, Conner always prodded his pupil into looking at a problem from every angle rather than from just one perspective and to consider all the alternatives. He explained that while a good leader always took his job seriously, he rarely took himself seriously. While George Patton had been a fellow student and peer for Eisenhower, Fox Conner became an invaluable mentor who could not only instruct him but also further his career.

Connor emphasized that the Versailles Peace Treaty terms made another war with Germany inevitable within a generation, that the United States would again be drawn into it, and that the commanders would have to learn how to work smoothly with allies. Conner contended that the commander-in-chief during World War I, the French leader General Ferdinand Foch, experienced difficulties with the allied nations because he lacked sufficient power over them. He argued that to avoid the same situation, the overall commander in the next war would have to insist on two items—adequate power and the willingness of the nations under his command to place their national interests in the background. Conner suggested that Eisenhower befriend another rising officer, George Marshall, because he had worked with the British and French allies in World War I and could share his expertise with him.

Although his mother had influenced the youngster in childhood, Conner shaped Eisenhower as a young man. "It is clear now that life with General Conner was a sort of graduate school in military affairs and the humanities, leavened by the comments and discourses of a man who was experienced in his knowledge of men and their conduct," Eisenhower wrote in 1967. Even after he had had the opportunity of associating with people on a world scale, including kings, diplomats, generals, and prime ministers, Eisenhower claimed that Conner "is the one more or less invisible figure to whom I owe an incalculable debt."[9]

After three years in Panama, Eisenhower returned to Camp Meade and again applied to the Infantry Advanced School at Fort Benning, but like his previous effort, his application was rejected. The chief of infantry still bristled over Eisenhower's advocacy of the tank and blocked his request. To reach the top ranks, Eisenhower had to attend both Fort Benning as well as the Command and General Staff School at Fort Leavenworth, stepping stones required for all officers seeking higher command. As long as Benning was denied him, he could go nowhere.

This time however, Eisenhower had someone in his corner. When Conner learned of Eisenhower's predicament, he sent a telegram alerting his protégé that he would soon receive a War Department order transferring him from the infantry to Colorado as an Army recruiter. This move out of the infantry was actually a demotion, but Eisenhower followed his mentor's wishes that he accept the transfer without question.

Conner arranged the move to shift Eisenhower into another branch of the army where the chief of infantry lacked influence. Conner knew that the army adjutant general, who controlled the recruiting branch to which Eisenhower now belonged, could name promising officers directly to Fort Leavenworth's school. Once Eisenhower had been properly transferred, in January 1925 Conner convinced the adjutant general to name Eisenhower to attend the Command and General Staff School.

An elated Eisenhower prepared to attend Leavenworth, but he wondered if the fact that he did not attend Fort Benning would slow his progress. Conner assured him that the three years he spent as his chief of staff, where he wrote the kind of reports they taught at Fort Benning, provided all the preparation Eisenhower needed.

His mentor knew what he was talking about. Eisenhower competed with 275 other officers in a rigorous course that tested their command skills. The army wanted to determine who could think under pressure, who could keep going even when they were tired and weary. The army had no way of placing young officers in battlefield conditions during peacetime, but Leavenworth simulated the exhaustion and intensity these men would face once in combat by working them long hours and putting them through rigorous field activities.

Despite the competition, Eisenhower finished first in his class, something he had never come close to at West Point. Eisenhower had bided his time until a true test of his abilities came along, and as far as the classroom was concerned, Leavenworth was by far a bigger challenge than West Point. Eisenhower was one of those individuals who rose to the occasion—the tougher the situation, the better he performed. West Point had been merely a preliminary phase he had to complete before facing a true test.

After his triumph at Leavenworth, Eisenhower received orders transferring him back to Fort Benning as executive officer, the second in command, of the 24th Infantry Regiment. Conner had again used his influence to have Eisenhower placed back in the infantry. With the Command and General Staff School on his resume, Eisenhower's prospects were bright.

He added another notch to his record in 1927 by attending the Army War College in Washington, D.C., which focused on the organization of armies and planning for wars. Attendees examined issues from a national perspective, and their solutions helped formulate army doctrine. As he had done at Leavenworth, Eisenhower graduated first in his class in June 1928.

In the late 1920s, before and after his time at the War College, he served on the American Battlefield Monuments Commission, a post that brought him into contact with General John J. Pershing, the army's most heralded officer. Eisenhower's task was to write a guidebook for the sites of World War I battles, an assignment that required him to spend time in Europe. This allowed him to familiarize himself with the terrain over which he would later command a vast army.

The 1920s had handed Eisenhower a series of challenging posts with Panama, Leavenworth, and Washington, D.C., and placed him in contact with influential men such as Conner and Pershing. These assignments and the associations paid off in the next decade, when Eisenhower steadily rose through the ranks.

CHAPTER 4

"A Brilliant Officer Should Be Promoted"

AT THE BEGINNING OF THE 1930S, THE FUTURE APPEARED BLEAK to the ambitious officer. Instead of being with soldiers, he was stuck in the nation's capital working in the War Department and with the army chief of staff. He had languished as a major since the early 1920s, and promotions in the small peacetime army, based largely on seniority, came slowly. Eisenhower's smile and good nature masked a burning desire to excel and to one day join the ranks of senior commanders.

His next task for the War Department in Washington was to research and write a mobilization plan outlining for American industry the transformation from a peacetime to a wartime economy. The project provided Eisenhower with valuable knowledge in an area that would be important to him during World War II and was meaningful for commanders of any war. He gained a thorough understanding of the complex relationship between a country's military and economic aims and examined successful methods for a smooth transition to a wartime footing.

Eisenhower traveled the nation to tour factories and interview industrial magnates, coming into contact with influential business leaders and understanding the connection between the military and the industrial realms. In his June 16, 1930, report to the War Department, Eisenhower stated that, "Our purpose is simple—to see to it that every individual and every material thing shall contribute, in the manner demanded by inherent characteristics, their full share to the winning of any war in which we may become involved."[1]

The report emphasized the need to be prepared economically and militarily so that when hostilities occurred, the United States could immediately deliver a powerful response. He wrote that "a reasonable preparation for defense is one of the best guarantees of peace. . . . The objective of any warring nation is victory, immediate and complete."[2]

Eisenhower addressed an issue that had surfaced throughout American history and continued into the next century. In times of peace, as had happened before World War I and as he faced in the 1930s, his nation lagged behind other countries in maintaining a potent military. Then, when war erupted, as it had in 1917 and would again in 1941 (and some would say, in 2001), the country labored furiously to meet the new challenge. Eisenhower urged that instead of such a haphazard approach, the United States should already have in place a plan to coordinate the military and industrial realms before a conflict brought about the necessity.

His report fell on deaf ears in the Herbert Hoover administration. The president explained that since he had no intentions of becoming involved in a conflict, the topic held no meaning for him.

The president may have ignored Eisenhower's study, but the army chief of staff, Douglas MacArthur, noticed it. He was impressed by Eisenhower's ability to compress such a complex issue into a concise summation, and he marveled over Eisenhower's talent for working with industrialists. As a result, MacArthur began to hand more writing assignments, such as speeches and reports, to his subordinate.

"Dear Eisenhower," MacArthur wrote after reading a report drafted by Eisenhower, "A magnificent effort on your part. Much better than I could have done myself." He later praised Eisenhower as being "well qualified for civilian contacts."[3]

In July of 1932, 20,000 World War I veterans gathered in Washington, D.C. to demand that a promised bonus to be paid in 1945 be immediately handed out instead. The veterans, labeled the Bonus Army by the press, felt doubly deprived during the Depression. Having sacrificed for their country, the veterans now faced the extra strain of having little hope for gainful employment in the deeply depressed economy. The United States had no unemployment policies and no social safety net at that time, and many thought that payment of the promised bonus would give the economy a modest boost. On July 28, when the local police attempted to move the men away from the Capitol, violence broke out. President Hoover ordered Army Chief of Staff MacArthur to move in army troops and reestablish order.

Eisenhower urged MacArthur to send a subordinate instead of personally taking charge of an action against veterans. He felt that it would be unseemly for an army chief of staff, bedecked in full uniform, to supervise the removal of war veterans. Given his eagerness to occupy center stage, MacArthur rejected the advice. His decision backfired. With MacArthur watching from nearby, the soldiers, including cavalry with drawn sabers, forced the veterans away from the Capitol. Onlookers shouted derogatory comments to the soldiers as they nudged the veterans back, and both MacArthur and the army received biting criticism from the nation's press for their roles.

"I told that dumb son-of-a-bitch he had no business going down there," explained a still-irate Eisenhower in an interview years later. "I told him it was no place for the Chief of Staff."[4]

Eisenhower's willingness to give blunt advice to MacArthur, along with his work in other posts, so impressed the general that he asked Eisenhower to join his staff. On February 20, 1933, MacArthur named him special assistant to the army chief of staff, and for the rest of the decade Eisenhower's fate was intertwined with that of MacArthur's.

MacArthur both astounded and perplexed Eisenhower. "On any subject he chose to discuss, his knowledge, always amazingly comprehensive, and largely accurate, poured out in a torrent of words," wrote an admiring Eisenhower. However, he then referred to MacArthur's penchant for dominating every conversation. "'Discuss' is hardly the correct word; discussion suggests dialogue and the General's conversations were usually monologues."[5]

As much as he admired MacArthur's genius and eloquence, Eisenhower noticed flaws in his superior. Eisenhower thought MacArthur was too eager to be the center of attention, and he found it arrogant that MacArthur often referred to himself in the third person. Eisenhower would later declare, only partly in jest, "I studied dramatics under him for five years in Washington and four years in the Philippines."[6]

On the other hand, Eisenhower admired MacArthur's determination to fight budgetary cutbacks for the army when politicians and much of the nation demanded a smaller military. MacArthur understood that repairing the ravaged economy took precedence over the needs of the military, but he refused to permit his army to be reduced to a mere shadow of itself. Even in tough economic times, the country needed a strong military as protection from foreign threats. No one could predict the time, method, or place of an attack, but as an officer, MacArthur wanted to be prepared.

Despite the barbs from powerful political opponents for his militaristic stance, MacArthur refused to back down. MacArthur frequently appeared before Congress to argue in behalf of increased military budgets, using reports and papers written by Eisenhower as preparation. It was as if he took any infringement on the nation's ability to defend itself personally. Eisenhower could relate to this single-mindedness.

While the two lived a complex relationship, Eisenhower was grateful for the experience he gained from MacArthur. Eisenhower's son, John, later wrote that MacArthur "showed his regard for Ike largely by the amount of work he was willing to pile on the younger officer, and the respect with which he usually listened to Ike's advice."[7] The numerous speeches and reports Eisenhower authored contained a wealth of information about the workings of the military and the industrial worlds. More importantly, members of Congress constantly contacted his office for military data and other information, giving Eisenhower familiarity in dealing with the political branch and placing him in touch with powerful leaders. The 1930s gave

Eisenhower the opportunity to practice the arts of persuasion and negotiation he would so dearly need in the 1940s.

When newspaper publisher William Randolph Hearst offered to triple Eisenhower's salary if he would leave MacArthur's office and become his top military correspondent, Eisenhower turned him down. He badly needed the money, but he recalled Fox Conner's words that the nation would one day be in a large European conflict. Fortunately for the country, Eisenhower felt an obligation to be there for his nation should the opportunity arise. Rarely can one find an individual who so burns with enthusiasm for his profession that he would spurn such a lucrative financial windfall, but that is precisely what Eisenhower did. The rejection of such an attractive proposal showed how devoted he was to the military, and while Hearst may have missed out on a talented correspondent, the nation reaped the benefits.

⊹╼╾⊹

In 1946, after four centuries of rule by Spain and then by the United States, the Philippines were due to obtain their independence. In 1935 the nation's president, Manuel Quezon, asked Douglas MacArthur to supervise the establishment and training of a Philippine army. MacArthur accepted and requested that Eisenhower accompany him. Eisenhower preferred to serve with troops and wanted to decline what would be another staff position with the general, but MacArthur insisted he needed Eisenhower. Reluctantly, Eisenhower acceded. Rather than making the lengthy trip to the Philippines, and recalling her unpleasant stay in Panama, Mamie remained in the United States until her husband could arrange for comfortable quarters.

Eisenhower and MacArthur faced nearly insurmountable difficulties in creating an effective Filipino fighting force. Not only did the Philippines lack sufficient funds to build an effective army but, caught in the throes of the Depression, the United States could provide little. Despite the obstacles, with the available funds MacArthur fielded a skeletal force, equipped it with outdated World War I-vintage weapons, and fashioned a workable defensive strategy.

The task of building a military in a distant land was immense, but Eisenhower quickly spotted the necessity for developing a friendly relationship with the host government and with the people. Behind the scenes, Eisenhower relied on his friendliness to smooth over any misunderstandings between MacArthur and Quezon, and on his inexhaustible energy to arrange training exercises for the Filipinos. Rather than ask Quezon to come to him, as MacArthur expected of the man he once called a "conceited little monkey,"[8] Eisenhower willingly met the Philippine leader in his office to discuss affairs, or aboard the president's yacht for an afternoon of bridge or fishing. Quezon responded to Eisenhower's affable nature and respect for him and his country.

MacArthur so appreciated Eisenhower's assistance that he wrote in an efficiency report that his aide was, "A brilliant officer . . . in time of war [he] should be promoted to general officer rank immediately."[9] Army superiors agreed. On July 1, 1936, Eisenhower was promoted to lieutenant colonel after almost sixteen years as a major.

Relations between Eisenhower and MacArthur deteriorated in 1937. MacArthur took umbrage when Eisenhower berated the general's decision in that year to accept from Quezon the position as field marshal of the Philippine army. Eisenhower had declined a similar offer to be a brigadier general, and when he learned of MacArthur's acceptance, he bluntly asked, "Why in the *hell* do you want a *banana* country giving you a field-marshal-ship?"[10] An irate MacArthur never forgot what he considered an impudent question.

A more serious issue arose over a planned military parade. To bring attention to the money-starved Filipino armed forces, MacArthur thought it would be a good idea to host an elaborate parade though Manila. He asked Eisenhower to start the arrangements.

When Quezon learned of this extravagance, he angrily demanded to know who was responsible for arranging something that would drain badly needed funds from his army. Eisenhower, who assumed Quezon had known of the planned parade, told him to contact MacArthur. When Quezon did, MacArthur claimed he knew nothing of the affair and stated that Eisenhower had simply been carried away in his enthusiasm for what was an obviously poor idea.

Eisenhower never again trusted MacArthur. He felt betrayed and believed that MacArthur had impugned his reputation. He asked MacArthur to send him home, but the general simply smiled, put his arm around him, and told him to forget the incident. "This misunderstanding caused considerable resentment," wrote Eisenhower in 1967, "and never again were we on the same warm and cordial terms."[11]

For much of his time in the Philippines, where he basically executed the orders drawn up by MacArthur, Eisenhower sought a way back into the infantry. He had been in the field with troops for only six months in his entire career, and he felt that if he were ever to advance, he needed more time with soldiers than with generals. That was not going to occur in the distant Philippines.

Every time he put in another transfer request, MacArthur blocked it, saying Eisenhower was too valuable to be released. Eisenhower employed every reason he could to persuade MacArthur to agree, sometimes going so far in what he said that he wondered why MacArthur did not fire him, but the general always refused. Eisenhower had become too adept at writing reports and organizing staffs.

Eisenhower accepted the situation with resignation, figuring that he would have to remain at least for the full four years' duration of his assignment. He was eager to leave, however, and knew MacArthur was aware of this. "However, from the beginning of this venture I've personally announced myself as ready and willing to go back to an assignment in the United States Army at any moment," he wrote in his diary after another failed request on July 9, 1937. "The general knows this if he knows anything, so I guess I don't have to make an issue of the matter by busting in and announcing it again."[12]

From contacts in and out of the military, the Jewish community in Manila heard of Eisenhower's expertise in organization. In 1938 the group offered him $60,000 a year, plus expenses, if he accepted a position assisting them in seeking an Asian location for Jewish refugees from Europe. The group's coordinators even guaranteed to place five years' salary in escrow, which would be paid to him should he leave before five years had expired. As with Hearst's offer, Eisenhower quickly rejected the deal. He could not bring himself to resign from the army, an institution that had supported his family and in which he had placed such faith.

Eisenhower had another reason for leaving when Major Richard D. Sutherland joined MacArthur's staff. A shameless self-promoter, Sutherland labored in the shadows to gain the confidence of the general while back-stabbing Eisenhower. When Eisenhower returned to Washington in 1938 to seek more financial assistance for the Philippines, Sutherland played up to MacArthur's vanity by constantly being at his beck and call and by telling him what a genius he was.

When Eisenhower returned to the Philippines in November 1938 he soon realized what Sutherland was doing and concluded that, for the sake of his own career, he had to return to the United States where he might possibly obtain command of an infantry outfit.

When war broke out in Europe in September 1939, Eisenhower saw yet another reason to leave the Philippines. It was not only that Eisenhower wanted to defend his nation. He felt he had the prime duty to destroy a single individual, the man most responsible for the craziness, a leader he labeled "a power-drunk egocentric"—Hitler. Eisenhower had closely followed the German leader's rise to power and had concluded that the man who constructed a government on fear had to be removed.

He wrote in his diary on the first day of war: "This evening we have been listening to broadcasts of [Neville] Chamberlain's speech stating that Great Britain was at war with Germany. After months and months of feverish effort to appease and placate the madman that is governing Germany the British and French seem to be driven into a corner out of which they can work their way only by fighting. It's a sad day for Europe and for the whole civilized world, though for a long time it has seemed ridiculous to refer to the world as civilized."

Eisenhower's anger rose with each word as he described Hitler's madness. "Hundreds of millions will suffer privations and starvation, millions will be killed and wounded because one man so wills it . . . Hitler's record with the Jews, his rape of Austria, of the Czechs, the Slovaks and now the Poles is as black as that of any barbarian of the Dark Ages."

Eisenhower concluded that he and every other freedom-loving individual must have one goal in mind when he added, "the final result will be that Germany will have to be dismembered and destroyed."[13] The war's purpose was simple to Eisenhower—rid the world of one man and many of its ills would disappear. Hitler was the evil protagonist who had to be annihilated.

Unlike the Korean and Vietnam conflicts, in which the enemy was not as clearly personified by one individual and distinctions between good and evil were blurred, Eisenhower and the nation benefited from the existence of a visible evil. Having defined that vile force, they could then turn all their efforts toward crushing it.

He finally convinced MacArthur to let him leave. Eisenhower believed that war for the United States was inevitable, and he wanted to be home when it started. As he later recounted, he said to MacArthur, "General, in my opinion the United States cannot remain out of this war for long. I want to go home as soon as possible. I want to participate in the preparatory work that I'm sure is going to be intense."[14] Eisenhower knew his chances of being a vital cog in any future war improved significantly if he were at home, closer to the power center, rather than thousands of miles away in the Philippines.

MacArthur agreed, perhaps influenced by his new-found reliance on Sutherland. President Quezon hated to lose such a valued officer and offered him a blank check if he stayed, but he also admired Eisenhower's loyalty to his nation.

On the last day of 1939, Eisenhower headed home, eager to serve. MacArthur accompanied him to the pier, where he presented Eisenhower with a bottle of Scotch whisky as a going-away present. What made Eisenhower happier, though, was the prospect of serving his country in perilous times. "I'm a soldier," he told Quezon at their final meeting. "I'm going home. We're going to war and I'm going to be in it."[15]

He had no idea how large a part of it he would become.

CHAPTER 5

"I Want People Who
Are Prepared to Fight"

THE ARMY EISENHOWER RETURNED TO WAS HARDLY CAPABLE OF instilling fear in its opponents, let alone defeat Hitler's vaunted forces. Every division faced shortages of manpower and equipment, the air arm boasted barely 1,000 aircraft, and the army did not possess a single armored division. As the German army tore through Poland, the United States military ranked a distant seventeenth in the world. Much work needed to be done to turn things around.

In January 1940, Eisenhower was named the commanding officer of the 1st Battalion, 15th Infantry operating out of Fort Lewis, Washington. This was the posting he had always wanted. He wasted no time placing his imprint on the soldiers, for he was more than ready to command troops in the field.

Eisenhower's command style was soon apparent. Rather than be confined to the dictates of army regulations, Eisenhower chose to rely on his judgment and common sense in dealing with the men. In explaining this attitude, he later boasted to a friend that he had never read *Army Regulations,* the manual so many other officers relied on for discipline of troops, and instead counted on proper assessment of a specific situation in making his decisions.

Once, two privates were fighting and needed to be disciplined. Instead of confining them to their quarters, Eisenhower ordered the pair to wash every window in the barracks. While one private cleaned the inside, his rival washed the outside of the same window. Initially, the two grimaced at each other and exchanged evil looks, but soon enough the grimaces turned into comical faces, then laughter. By day's end the privates had forgotten their disputes, harmony had been restored to the battalion, and the men began to realize that in Eisenhower, they had a unique officer.

On another occasion, while inspecting a kitchen, Eisenhower grabbed a large handful of uncooked ground beef and an onion, and ate the food raw as he completed his inspection. "By God, *there's* a tough guy!"[1] thought the cook who quickly spread word throughout the battalion. Eisenhower's men saw that their new officer was not only imaginative with his discipline, but accustomed to making do with whatever was at hand rather than demand normal amenities.

Eisenhower could be tough, but he also insisted on fairness from himself and every other officer in his command. One morning he asked a private to hand him the score book registering the young man's performance in a weapons-firing activity. When the private replied that he did not have it, Eisenhower headed straight for the soldier's platoon leader, Lieutenant Burton S. Barr. The officer never knew what hit him, as Eisenhower unleashed a torrent of profanity-laced words castigating the officer for not maintaining proper records .

"I've heard about being eaten out, and I've seen it, but this was unique," Barr recalled later. "This wasn't being eaten out. This was Eisenhower having a buffet supper, and I was the complete meal."

Eisenhower wanted the lieutenant to understand his duties, and more importantly, to realize that everyone makes mistakes and must learn from them. That is why later in the day Eisenhower again chatted with Barr and explained why he had chewed him out. As long as the officer benefited from the incident and failed to repeat the same mistake, Eisenhower was content to let the matter rest. As the discussion ended, Eisenhower added that the incident was over. "That was the end. We don't carry grudges around here,"[2] he told Barr.

Now that he finally had his battalion, Eisenhower wanted it to be the best in the army. He drilled and trained the men every day, all day, and kept telling them that with a war coming soon, their chances of survival rose as they became more proficient in training. Errors made during practice instead of on the battlefield saved lives, he contended, and thus he insisted his officers and men be assiduously attentive to their tasks.

Eisenhower was not one of those officers who issued orders, then disappeared while others carried them out. He worked harder than any other man, eighteen hours a day, seven days a week, and rarely slept more than a handful of hours.

Perhaps what most set Eisenhower apart from his fellow officers was his realization that if he were able to adequately prepare his men for combat, they had to understand the reasons for training and for fighting. People in a democracy demand explanations. Without them the effort noticeably slackens; with them the workload soars. "Americans either will not or cannot fight at maximum efficiency unless they understand the why and wherefore of their orders,"[3] he stated. Consequently, he issued clear orders, gave the reasons for them to his officers, and then expected the officers to relay that information to the men on the line.

History offers numerous examples, such as the American Revolution, in which soldiers who understand the reasons for their conflict fight with more purpose. History also presents instances, such as Vietnam, in which the reasons for going to war are not as clear-cut. A dictator does not have to worry about the rationale for sending men into combat, but Eisenhower grasped the important concept that to pull the most out of soldiers in a democracy, he had to become a teacher and explain situations to them.

Eisenhower spent as much time in the field as he did at the office. He received a welcome surge of freshness and vitality from visiting the soldiers—a stuffy office had never been right for him—and he used the time to learn their concerns and to educate them about their roles. He claimed that morale was most severely harmed by neglect and favoritism, so he spent much of his day making sure the troops did not feel that way. He personally observed many maneuvers and drills, and mingled with the troops whenever possible. Eisenhower did not want to be an indifferent commander who acted as if a huge gulch stood between him and his men.

His rigorous training had one other reason—to learn which officers and men could perform well under strain and which needed to be replaced. The demands of war are sometimes too great for individuals. Eisenhower wanted to learn who those men were and bring in substitutes before he had to lead them into battle.

"If any of you think we are not going to war, I don't want you in my battalion," he told his officers, mindful of Fox Conner's words. "We're going to war. This country is going to war, and I want people who are prepared to fight that war."[4]

"I am having the time of my life,"[5] Eisenhower wrote to a West Point classmate about his time with the troops. If it were up to him, he would never again see the interior of a staff office. The men responded to Eisenhower with equal fervor. They so admired his fairness and thoroughness in training that after a while, the only song the battalion would march to was "Beer Barrel Polka," Eisenhower's favorite. They sensed that this officer had not chosen the army for fame or glory, as had some of Eisenhower's peers. He served to help make them better soldiers who, in turn, would better serve the nation.

By 1940 Eisenhower had developed a series of principles that showed his farsightedness and helped convince superiors that he was a man to watch. Once Eisenhower was convinced of an idea's worth, he promoted it at every chance, no matter how many obstacles stood in his way. In the early 1920s, for instance, he did not abandon his advocacy of the tank until ordered to by a superior officer.

"So be self-confident," he advised his seventeen-year-old son, John, in a May 10, 1940 letter, "when your own conscience tells you you've studied a matter out honestly and well, stick by your conclusions, and if necessary to act on them, do so fearlessly." He warned his son, however, to avoid alienating others with an overzealous advocacy of a cause. Persuasion, Eisenhower believed, came from sound logic and organized thought, not dramatics. "But merely because one has an opinion," he added to John, "he doesn't have to shout it from the housetops . . ."[6]

Eisenhower relentlessly advanced the idea that war approached, and that the military had to prepare both the country's populace and the military. Given Eisenhower's ability to clearly explain the reasons behind orders to the troops, it fell to him and others in the services, such as Patton, to clearly delineate the threat posed by Hitler. On November 26, 1940, he wrote to his friend Everett Hughes, "We may not be at war now . . . but how can we eventually avoid it? . . . The American population, once it gets truly irritated, is a self-confident, reckless, fast-moving avalanche . . . And it is *our* job to speed up the preparatory forces!"[7] More than most of his contemporaries, he saw that the public had to understand the threat, and when it did, the military had to be ready to act quickly.

To achieve this, Eisenhower contended that every officer had to do his part in readying his troops for war. "I was never more serious in my life than I am about the need for each of us, particularly in the Regular Army, to do his whole chore intelligently and energetically," he wrote a friend in November 1940. "The thing that worries me most is the seeming lassitude, and the apparent indifference to the existing international situation, that is displayed by so many of our officers . . . if ever we are to prove that we're worth the salaries the government has been paying us all these years—now is the time!"[8]

Eisenhower's words are especially relevant for the first part of the twenty-first century, when the United States faced a terrorist threat from abroad. Whether apathy and a lack of knowledge about world situations by the citizenry and the military in any way contributed to mayhem in Baghdad after Saddam Hussein's fall or to the Abu Ghraib controversy is a matter for conjecture, but a prepared, educated army and citizenry, as

Eisenhower intended for the men he commanded, might have led to different results.

With what he saw as an unavoidable conflict with Germany approaching, Eisenhower maintained that the army had to ruthlessly wean itself of incompetent officers, as mistakes made by commanders translate to a learning experience in training but to deaths on the battlefield. As he wrote to Brigadier General Leonard T. Gerow, the chief of the War Plans Division, on September 25, 1941, "One of the things that is causing the greatest trouble is that of eliminating unfit officers, of all grades and of all components. It is a hard thing to do, and in many cases it is too hard for some of the people in charge. But it is a job that has got to be done."[9]

Along this line, Eisenhower believed that an officer had to think of his men and his nation above personal considerations. Eisenhower stated that wars do not allow for a narrow-minded approach in which an officer focuses on advancing his own career first and looks to the preparation of his men second. If an officer failed to think of his men and duties, he would soon be replaced, because wars "bring to the top the fellow who thinks more of his job than of his own promotion prospects."[10]

Unlike some of his brethren in the Regular Army who thought that only West Point graduates should receive commands, Eisenhower saw no problem in promoting a National Guard officer over one from the Regular Army. Quality and capabilities counted to him, not a man's route into the service. He wrote on October 24, 1941, to Joel F. Carlson, Mamie's uncle, about this issue and stated that, "the safety of the country, and the lives of their sons and brothers are possibly going to be at stake! So let's stop talking of classes and of castes. We must see what the job is, and we must insist on getting people who can do it, and we shouldn't give a hoot whether he is Regular or National Guard. He merely must do the job *right*—or get out! We cannot safely tolerate ineptitude, ignorance, inexperience." Eisenhower ended the letter by declaring that, "the need is so great in every position from 2nd lieutenant to general for moral courage, military efficiency, and self-sacrifice. And far too often, these are hard to find."[11]

Eisenhower learned that to have the most proficient military possible, a commander had to select the best-qualified men. Their popularity with fellow officers, their education and background, their path into the military—none of it mattered beside the desire to fashion an effective fighting unit from the men he commanded.

⫘⊷⊶⫘

In the fall of 1940 Eisenhower's hopes soared when George Patton wrote to him that he hoped to name him a regimental commander in a new armored division he was about to form. But superiors had other designs for Eisenhower. Lieutenant General Walter Krueger, commander of the Third Army at Fort Sam Houston, saw Eisenhower as the perfect selection as his chief of staff. On June 11, 1941 Krueger wrote U.S. Army Chief of Staff George Marshall that the job required "A man possessing broad vision, progressive ideas, a thorough grasp of the magnitude of the problems involved in handling an army, and lots of initiative and resourcefulness."[12] Eisenhower was his man.

That November, despite vigorous objections, Eisenhower left the 15th Infantry to become chief of staff of the 3rd Division. So upset over the move away from commanding men, he developed a case of shingles, and he wrote everybody he could think of in an attempt to avoid the shift, but to no avail. Eisenhower once again was behind a desk rather than with the troops in the field, and again faced the prospect of missing out on combat. "So again I'm looking down a pen instead of a gun,"[13] a miserable Eisenhower wrote a friend. Eisenhower would gladly abandon future promotions if he could only remain with his beloved 15th Infantry.

The Third Army was twice the size of Civil War general Ulysses S. Grant's largest army. It took Eisenhower out of field command, but it handed him excellent experience in strategy and tactics for his later role in Europe. The army had expanded to 1,500,000 men by mid-1941, but it lacked any test to determine its capabilities. To remedy this, the army scheduled a vast September 1941 military maneuver in Louisiana, pitting 160,000 troops of the Second Army against 240,000 soldiers of the Third Army. As Krueger's chief of staff, the task of planning the Third Army's moves in what became the largest peacetime military exercise in American history fell to Eisenhower. "Like a vast laboratory experiment, the maneuvers would prove the worth of ideas, men, weapons, and equipment,"[14] he later wrote.

Eisenhower maintained open communications with his officers. Every morning, he met with his unit commanders to discuss the positives and negatives of the previous day. He wanted to make sure the men understood what errors had been made and, more importantly, how to avoid them in the future. "We had to uncover and highlight every mistake, every failure, every foulup that in war could be death to a unit or an army."[15]

Unlike most of his colleagues, Eisenhower also realized the value of the press in military matters. He understood the importance of having the public's support in a democracy, and one way of obtaining that support was to establish a friendly relationship with the men and women who disseminate news. Thus, each morning during the maneuvers, Eisenhower helmed a question-and-answer session with a group of military correspondents. The writers appreciated Eisenhower's ability to lucidly explain military tactics, and they quickly warmed to his affable grin and easygoing manner. The correspondents were surprised to learn that Eisenhower never tried to sugar-coat anything. If the maneuver showed a deficiency, Eisenhower did not hide it. If he explained the military's shortcomings to the press, they in turn could convey to the nation what the military needed to do to be ready for any fighting. First among the officers from his West Point class, Eisenhower recognized the value of positive public relations and how much the press can help or hinder a man's career.

Slowly, Eisenhower's name began appearing in the nation's press coverage. Drew Pearson, one of the nation's top columnists, wrote that Colonel Eisenhower "conceived and directed the strategy that routed the Second Army." He added that Eisenhower "has a steel-trap mind plus unusual physical vigor [and] to him the military profession is a science and he began watching and studying the German Army five years ago."[16]

An irate General Krueger, on the other hand, dismissed Eisenhower's warm relationship with the press as an attempt to further his own career at the expense of Krueger's. He believed that Eisenhower usurped much of the credit for the successful maneuvers, spent an inordinate amount of time promoting himself with the press, and made sure his name appeared in the headlines more frequently than the general's.

The Third Army readily dismantled the Second Army in the Louisiana maneuvers, almost capturing the opposing commander in the process. Eisenhower claimed that the maneuvers illuminated shortcomings in men, supplies, and tactics, and brought the most capable leaders to the forefront. Later, he also stated that the maneuvers on the fields of Louisiana provided him and other officers indispensable experience for the 1944 race across France.

After the maneuvers, the army ruthlessly purged its ranks of the incompetent. Hundreds of senior officers were forced into retirement. Of 42 corps and division commanders, 31 were relieved, as well as 20 of 27 division commanders. At the same time, a handful of officers rose in prominence, chief among them Eisenhower and Patton.

When Eisenhower received a promotion to brigadier general on October 3, 1941, the proud officer feared only one thing—that he had performed so capably for Krueger in the maneuvers that he might never again leave a staff position and enjoy a combat command. He rarely spoke of this to anyone, however, as he only wanted to serve where he was most needed.

His worries appeared to be justified when George Marshall asked Brigadier General Mark Clark, a rising star in the army, to submit a list of ten officers for consideration as head of the Operations Division. Clark explained he only needed one name—Eisenhower's. "If you have to have ten names," he told Marshall, "I'll just put nine ditto marks below."[17]

⊹═══⊹

On December 7, 1941 Eisenhower read reports and answered letters at his Fort Sam Houston office until noon. When he finished, he told his staff he was returning to his quarters for a nap and that he was not to be disturbed unless a matter of extreme urgency arose. He had barely drifted off to sleep when Mamie awakened him with the news that the Japanese had bombed the American military bases and airfields at Pearl Harbor in Hawaii. "Well, boys, it's come,"[18] Eisenhower said when he returned to his office.

Eisenhower spent the next five days preparing his men for a hasty transfer to the West Coast, which was then thought to be in danger of a Japanese assault. Eager to be with his fellow American soldiers as they faced combat, Eisenhower worked day and night to ready the Third Army.

On December 12, however, Colonel Walter Bedell "Beetle" Smith of the War Department called him with instructions from Marshall to hop on the next airplane and fly to Washington, D.C. Eisenhower figured this meant his chances of an immediate field command were over and he called the message "a hard blow." He had missed the fighting in World War I, and now with the nation facing one of its most severe crises in history, he was relegated to the nation's capital. He gloomily assumed it meant "a virtual repetition of my experience in World War I. Heavy-hearted, I telephoned my wife to pack a bag, and within the hour I was headed for the War Department."[19]

Little did Eisenhower know that, instead of languishing on the sidelines of history, he stood on the verge of greatness.

CHAPTER 6

"The Unexpected Always Happens"

EISENHOWER ARRIVED IN WASHINGTON ON DECEMBER 14 AND immediately headed to George Marshall's office. Marshall described the bleak situation in the Pacific, where Japanese armed forces had launched attacks against many Allied territories. Their assaults included Wake Island and the Philippines, where they all but eliminated the meager American air power that existed in the Pacific. He then asked Eisenhower what he would do if he were commander in the Far East. Eisenhower left the room to organize his thoughts.

After a few hours Eisenhower returned and outlined his position. He stated that because Japan held the upper hand almost everywhere else in the Pacific, the most crucial task facing the United States was to build a base of operations in Australia. He believed that a Japanese victory in the

Philippines was imminent, but that the United States could not simply withdraw its forces or cease rushing men and supplies to the islands. Such a drastic move would send the wrong signal to the people of Asia, who "may excuse failure but they will not excuse abandonment." Marshall listened to the advice, then told Eisenhower, "Do your best to save them."[1]

Marshall then added a cautionary statement. "Eisenhower, the [War] Department is filled with able men who analyze their problems well but feel compelled always to bring them to me for final solution. I must have assistants who will solve their own problems and tell me later what they have done."[2]

Marshall dropped Eisenhower into a political and military maelstrom. At this stage of the war, reference to the Philippines meant one thing—MacArthur. The Japanese had caught Eisenhower's former superior with his defenses down, causing MacArthur to oversee what would quickly become a swift retreat to the Bataan Peninsula. Most likely to mask his embarrassment, MacArthur hounded the War Department for additional men and supplies, claiming that he could not stave off defeat with the meager allotment currently in the Pacific and that the United States was honor-bound to protect the Philippines.

Eisenhower became Marshall's front man in dealing with MacArthur. He handled MacArthur's requests and, while he attempted to shift as many resources as possible to the beleaguered forces, he usually had to tell the general that the militarily-strapped nation could do little to aid him. Overall strategy called for the defeat of Germany first while American forces in the Pacific went on the defensive. As these were arguments that the insistent MacArthur did not want to hear, Eisenhower spent much of his time handling his complaints.

"Tempers are short," he wrote in his diary on January 4, 1942, after less than a month on the job. "There are lots of amateur strategists on the job, and prima donnas everywhere. I'd give anything to be back in the field."[3]

But combat in the field was not meant to be. He would be stuck in an office for the foreseeable future, trying to send whatever help he could to the Philippines while biting his lip over MacArthur's vicious criticisms. The general knew Eisenhower could do little—the country had precious little to send, few ships with which to transport it, and the Japanese enjoyed air supremacy in the region—but that did not end his caustic comments about the War Department's abandonment of the Philippines.

Eisenhower understood the importance of the situation, which seemed custom designed for the publicity-seeking MacArthur. He wrote in his diary on February 23 that, "Bataan is made to order for him. It's in the public eye; it has made him a public hero; it has all the essentials of drama; and he is the acknowledged king on the spot." Eisenhower added that at this time, "there has got to be a lot of patience—no one person can be a Napoleon or a Caesar . . . It's a backbreaking job to get a simple battle order out, and then it can't be executed for from three to four months."[4] He claimed that with his never-ending stream of requests, MacArthur was acting like a baby who was not getting what he wanted.

Eisenhower spent many hours agonizing over his inability to adequately reinforce the troops in the Philippines. He understood that he was not trying to prevent a defeat in the islands, just to delay it, but that only made his task more difficult. He knew many of the officers then fighting for their lives in the Philippines; that he could do little to help close friends haunted him. Mamie watched at night as her husband paced the room fretting over the lack of resources, repeating, "Dear God, I don't have it. I don't have it to send."[5]

Eisenhower endured the frustrations that faced officers in every war who labored to provide adequate material to the man on the front line. Unfortunately, the nation had not maintained a well-supplied military through the years of peace. Now that war had started, the country had to make do with what it had on hand until American factories could produce the necessary weapons and supplies. Sadly, the infantryman suffered most for this lack of foresight. Conditions in 2005 illustrated a similar phenomenon, as American forces in Iraq suffered from a lack of armor plating for their vehicles.

Despite the close ties to friends in the Philippines, by late January Eisenhower argued more persuasively that the war effort had to be expanded in Europe, even at the cost of reducing the already meager flow of supplies heading to Australia. Hitler posed the greater threat, and with the Soviet Union reeling from a German invasion, materials had to be sent to the Soviet ally to keep them in the war. Two months on the job had given Eisenhower a better appreciation for the overall picture. When Eisenhower examined the military situation on a global scale, he could not help but conclude that first Hitler, then the Japanese, had to be stopped.

At Marshall's request, former Secretary of War Patrick J. Hurley traveled to Australia to assess the situation in the Far East. After meeting with officials, he concluded neither Eisenhower nor anyone else could do much. "We were out-shipped, out-planed, out-maneuvered, and out-gunned by the Japanese from the beginning."[6]

In mid-February the aircraft tender *Langley* transported 32 aircraft to the Far East. As the ship steamed near Java and within range of Japanese air power, the Japanese attacked the carrier, sinking it and all 32 aircraft. Eisenhower's frustration as well as his contention that little could be done to save the Philippines mounted.

In March, President Roosevelt ordered MacArthur to flee the Philippines and establish an Allied headquarters in Australia. Finally, Eisenhower's trying three-month Philippine ordeal ended. Now involved in a world war, Eisenhower had gained valuable experience in dealing with commanders, arranging supplies, and assessing matters on a global scale. He was beginning to learn that the viewpoint of the United States and its needs were not necessarily the only ones requiring consideration.

By this time, Eisenhower also had his first encounter with the British allies at a series of meetings that brought Winston Churchill and top British officials to Washington, D.C. from late December until mid-January. Some of the Americans were suspicious of their British counterparts, whose primary concern was the safety and preservation of the British Empire, but Eisenhower, having benefited from his Philippine endeavor, was able to work with the British. He undoubtedly recalled Fox Conner's advice that in the next war, a commander would have to show agility in working with allies.

+━━━+

The British were not alone in appreciating Eisenhower's work. George Marshall, who did not suffer fools and readily reassigned any officer who could not perform, warmed to Eisenhower's organizational talent and devotion to the army. On February 16, 1942, he named Eisenhower his chief plans and operations officer, an influential post he would hold until June. As such, Eisenhower would be responsible for drawing up the military plans for the entire army.

Still hoping for a field command, Eisenhower tried to argue his way out of the new staff assignment. He told his boss that other generals had recommended him for command of a division, which both Eisenhower and Marshall knew was the fastest route to promotion, but Marshall would not be dissuaded. He told Eisenhower that despite his disappointment, he was going to remain in war plans and he did not want to hear about the issue anymore.

"General, I'm interested in what you say, but I want you to know that I don't give a damn about your promotion plans as far as I'm concerned," Eisenhower spat back. "I came into this office from the field and I am trying to do my duty. I expect to do so as long as you want me here. If that locks me to a desk for the rest of the war, so be it!"[7]

Few people, let alone a staff officer, spoke to Marshall in that manner, but Eisenhower got away with it. Marshall expected Eisenhower to accept his posting like a good soldier, but appreciated that the officer stood up for himself and made it clear that he would prefer a field command. In what had to be incredibly frustrating to Eisenhower, the man he replaced in war plans received a field command. Eisenhower could take solace in at least having been named a major general.

As head of war plans for the American military around the world, Eisenhower supervised a staff of more than one hundred officers and orchestrated a worldwide strategy that required him to examine all points of view—those of the Allies as well as every branch of the U.S. military. He told his staff that he did not want any man to dismiss another staff member's plan until that man had formulated an alternative strategy to replace it and was able to completely explain the reasons for the action. Straight rejections accomplished little more than to disillusion the person promoting the proposal and make him less willing to submit future ideas. Eisenhower wanted every idea to be considered and replaced only by better plans.

By late March Eisenhower and his staff had developed the first drafts of what eventually became the European campaign against Hitler. The first segment, called Roundup, earmarked 5,800 aircraft and 48 infantry and armored divisions for an April 1, 1943, assault against the mainland between Le Havre and Boulogne. A second part, named Bolero, consisted of amassing in the British Isles the men and material required for a subsequent major cross-channel attack against the French coast. Finally, Eisenhower supervised the planning of Sledgehammer, an emergency attack along the European coastline should the collapse of the Soviet Union appear likely.

Eisenhower's work brought him into frequent and often exasperating contact with the British and with high-ranking U.S. Navy officers, each of whom sought something for his own purposes. He scribbled in his diary after a particularly arduous day dealing with competing demands, "Fox Conner was right about allies. He could well have included the navy."[8]

Eisenhower had particular difficulties dealing with the chief of naval operations, Admiral Ernest J. King, an irascible commander who thought of the navy first and last. "We're having our troubles in joint army-navy problems," Eisenhower confided to his diary on February 23. "Admiral King . . . is an arbitrary, stubborn type, with not too much brains and a tendency toward bullying his juniors."[9]

Marshall sent Eisenhower to King's office to discuss an important issue. When Eisenhower walked in, the admiral barely looked up at him. King permitted Eisenhower to present his case, then without lifting his head, rejected the army's contention. Instead of leaving, which is what most junior officers would have done, Eisenhower remained in the office and told King he was disrespectful in so hastily dismissing Marshall's ideas. A surprised King looked up at Eisenhower, waited a few seconds, then asked him to repeat his arguments. This time King listened and changed his mind. Eisenhower left the officer with a greater respect for King.

Eisenhower's long days taxed his stamina. He rarely enjoyed more than a few hours rest, and Mamie might as well have been living on the moon. Lucian K. Truscott Jr., a close friend and one of the war's most able commanders, spent a day in Eisenhower's office during a visit to Washington and was amazed at the constant demands for Eisenhower's attention. An endless stream of people poured into his office, each demanding something or seeking a solution to a problem, and according to Truscott, "Every view was considered. Each problem was carefully analyzed." Truscott added that Eisenhower had the "extraordinary ability to place his finger at once upon the crucial fact in any problem or the weak point in any proposition . . . [and] to arrive at quick and confident decisions."[10]

Eisenhower's driver, Mickey McKeogh, picked him up in late February after not having seen him for a while and was stunned at how he had changed. "The first thing I thought was that he was more tired than I'd ever seen him; all of his face was tired . . . His voice was tired, like his face. He got in the car without saying much of anything and all the way back to the hotel he said almost nothing."[11]

He felt so tied to his job that on March 10, when his father died, Eisenhower did not even return to Abilene. He claimed that war duties demanded his full attention, but his failure to go home reflects more on the distant relationship he had had with his father than on his attitude toward his responsibilities. The only indication of how much this death affected Eisenhower was that he closed his office door for thirty minutes on March 12, the day his father was buried. In his diary he wrote that he felt horrible he could not be with his mother.

In these early months of 1942, Eisenhower fretted over not being in the field. His friend George Patton came through with timely encouragement. He wrote, "I have the utmost confidence that through your efforts we will eventually beat the hell out of those bastards—'You name them; I'll shoot them!'" When Eisenhower replied that he would most likely not witness much shooting, stuck as he was behind a desk, Patton admonished, "Ike, don't give up. The basic truth of war is that the unexpected always happens. It will be a long war. We'll get together yet."[12]

On June 21, 1942, Eisenhower met with the British prime minister, Winston Churchill. The noted leader was eating lunch with presidential adviser Harry Hopkins when Hopkins mentioned that the president, Franklin Delano Roosevelt, wanted him to meet two promising officers. Eisenhower and Mark Clark entered the room, and the quartet chatted about Roundup for an hour. "I was immediately impressed by these remarkable but hitherto unknown men," wrote Churchill after the war. "I felt sure that these officers were intended to play a great part in it [Roundup], and that was the reason why they had been sent to make my acquaintance."[13]

Seeing Eisenhower's immense promise, Marshall did whatever he could to make him known to top political and military leaders from both the United States and Great Britain. He handed Eisenhower vast responsibility with the war plans job and asked him to participate in the Arcadia conference, a January 1942 meeting of top Allied political and military figures who gathered to set strategy against Japan and Germany. Marshall would not have done either unless he had spotted talent in Eisenhower, for Marshall was never one to let an unqualified officer remain at his post. As historian Stephen Ambrose wrote, Marshall searched for men who possessed the willingness to take responsibility on their own shoulders, who viewed situations optimistically and confidently, who hated to draw attention to themselves, who could work with the British, and who adopted aggressive strategies. Eisenhower fit the bill in every aspect.

At the same time, Eisenhower studied Marshall's techniques and absorbed what he thought was useful. A politician once telephoned Marshall, but the general abruptly ended the conversation when he realized the man only wanted to recommend a certain officer for promotion. He told the influential politician that he despised such patronage and would go out of his way to ensure the man was not advanced. Eisenhower learned that an officer sometimes had to stand up to prominent individuals, a lesson he later employed with Roosevelt and Churchill.

Eisenhower also liked the way that Marshall gave his staff assignments, then allowed them to do their work with minimal interference. Unlike some commanders, Marshall enjoyed being surrounded by men who had the confidence to disagree with him. He believed that such individuals guaranteed he would hear all sides of different issues.

The only flaw Eisenhower noticed with Marshall was that his brusque manner seemed to intimidate many officers. Eisenhower watched qualified men stammer and have difficulty expressing their opinions in front of the general because they feared his reaction. Eisenhower preferred a less aggressive approach that would permit a freer exchange of views. Aside from this, Eisenhower considered Marshall one of the major influences in his life.

Later, in October 1942, he would write that he would not trade one Marshall for fifty MacArthurs.

⊣══⊨

In late May 1942 Marshall sent Eisenhower to London to find out why the buildup in American forces was proceeding so slowly. Eisenhower quickly uncovered an abysmal lack of organization and effort; officers barely worked eight hours a day and took every weekend off. Eisenhower drew up a list of suggestions for Marshall.

Eisenhower renewed acquaintances with members of the British command. He generally made a favorable impression although he and General Bernard Montgomery experienced a rocky start. When Eisenhower walked into Montgomery's office for a military briefing, the British officer pompously asserted that he was only taking time from his busy schedule because he had been ordered to. He then started talking, at which point Eisenhower lit a cigarette. Montgomery stopped his presentation to inform Eisenhower that, in his offices, smoking was not permitted. Eisenhower quietly snuffed out the cigarette without remark but later exploded to an American associate and called Montgomery a son-of-a-bitch. Though Eisenhower remained distant with the British commander throughout the war, he tried not to let this awkward introduction color his judgment.

Eisenhower returned to Washington in early June to submit his findings to Marshall. He argued that unless drastic changes were made, including relieving the commanding officer, the schedule for military operations was in jeopardy. He added that whoever took over had to be able to work with the British as an equal partner, and he asked Marshall to seriously study his recommendations if he wanted to spark action.

"I certainly do want to read it," answered Marshall. "You may be the man who executes it. If that's the case, when can you leave?"[14]

The unexpected question startled Eisenhower, but he gathered his composure and replied he could be ready at any time. On June 11, three days after the meeting, Marshall named Eisenhower as commander of the European Theater of Operations. Everyone, including Eisenhower, assumed he would remain in the post until the spring of 1943, when

Marshall would take command for the cross-channel assault, but for a time, at least, Eisenhower would operate from the field and have a direct influence on the war.

"The chief of staff says I'm the guy," wrote an ecstatic Eisenhower in his diary that day. "Now we really go to work."[15] He had labored day and night in war plans for six months, and now he had the chance to make a mark where he felt it counted—with the troops. Other than his brief time with the 15th Infantry, Eisenhower had spent little time in the field, but he had continued to view any post as a classroom in which he could learn the techniques of command. For six months he worked at the side of George Marshall, collaborated with the British, and handled powerful politicians. He may have been less experienced than others, but he was ready.

He headed home for dinner with Mamie. As the couple ate and shared the events of the day, Eisenhower casually announced that he had to return to London.

"What post are you going to have?" she asked her husband.

"I'm going to command the whole shebang."[16]

PART III

First Commands

✛═✛

CHAPTER 7

"We're Here to Fight"

On June 23, 1942, Mamie Eisenhower stood by the Fort Myer flagpole and watched the aircraft taking her husband to Europe lift off the runway. Normally she would not have been there, but her husband had specifically asked her to wait beside the flagpole so that he could see her when the airplane flew overhead. The image represented the two most important factors in Eisenhower's life—flag and family—and he now headed overseas to defend both.

Eisenhower arrived in London the following day to take command of the European Theater of Operations, U. S. Army (ETOUSA). Headquartered at 20 Grosvenor Square, his offices soon became known as "Eisenhowerplatz" by soldiers and officers.

Eisenhower found himself in the middle of a political and military morass. Ostensibly fighting to protect democracy, he had to work with a colonial empire, Great Britain, and a communist dictatorship, the Soviet Union. The redeeming feature was that the three nations shared a common goal—to remove Hitler from power as soon as possible. With Eisenhower's single-minded determination to crush the German leader, the Allies had the right man in command.

Eisenhower wasted little time establishing his imprint on operations. On June 25, during the first meeting with his staff, Eisenhower was surprised to notice an air of negativity and indifference in the room. The British fretted over the loss of Tobruk in North Africa and 30,000 British soldiers in North Africa four days earlier to General Erwin Rommel, and the U.S. officers at headquarters seemed to focus on entertainment and relaxation more than on the myriad problems they faced. He decided he had to quickly establish a new mood.

"Pessimism and defeatism will not be tolerated," he told a hushed staff. "Any officer or soldier who cannot rise above the obstacles and bitter prospects that lie in store for us has no recourse but to ask for instant release from this theater. And if he shows such attitude and doesn't ask for release, he will go home anyway."

To emphasize his point, he reminded the men, "We're here to fight and not to be wined and dined."[1]

Eisenhower explained that he sought every officer's input, and they should thus feel free to bring their ideas to his attention. This was not to be a headquarters ruled by formality and rigidity, but one of free discussion. Above all, he wanted them to handle their own problems and only take to their superior those issues they lacked the power or resources to solve.

The officers left that meeting with a renewed sense of purpose and with an enthusiasm that spread to those around them. At Grosvenor Square, resolve and exertion had replaced lackadaisical effort and poisonous attitudes. Kay Summersby, a British driver who frequently chauffeured Eisenhower about London, wrote that Grosvenor Square "had once been rather a social center; we went to work around 10 in the morning, took an hour and a half for lunch, knocked off about teatime in the afternoon. Now it was run strictly on military lines. Headquarters had been reorganized. Instead of the easygoing group of 'observers' whose schedules included long liquid lunches and early cocktail hours, 20 Grosvenor Square was peopled by army men . . . on a seven-day week. General Eisenhower had come over to do a job; he was wasting no time."[2]

Eisenhower's changes did not stop with headquarters. More than most commanders, Eisenhower empathized with the privates and corporals at the front more than he did with generals and prime ministers. He felt a contentment and peace with them that he rarely attained in the circles of high command. He considered his work with the 15th Infantry his most rewarding service to date, so it was no surprise that one of his initial actions in Great Britain was to visit the men who were about to head into battle.

One way of replacing defeatism with enthusiasm was to show the soldiers about to enter combat that he cared. In a June 26, 1942, letter to George Marshall, Eisenhower explained why he wanted to be with the bomber crews soon to fly the first air attack by Americans against the Germans. "Thirty of our officers and men will take part soon in a secret operation. I deeply regret that my better judgment compels me to refrain from participating myself. I am going to see each of the thirty, individually, before D-day, and if it is humanly possible I am going to greet each one personally upon his return. I hope you will not be astonished if I deal out decorations rather generously on that occasion. I believe it will have a tremendous moral effect, particularly because the occasion will mark the first offensive action by Americans in this theater in this war."[3]

Eisenhower then turned his attention to the third group whose cooperation he needed—the press. As he had done during the Louisiana maneuvers, throughout the war Eisenhower made sure the press was well informed. He knew that they were his conduit to the American people and that they could help convey valuable information to the nation.

He held his first press conference only one day after arriving in London, at which time he told the reporters he considered them a part of his staff and that he would divulge whatever information he could safely impart. His aides observed Eisenhower create an instant bond with the group, and from that time forward, he had the press in his corner.

One aide, Captain Harry Butcher, who witnessed this first press conference, concluded that Eisenhower would have little trouble with the reporters. "Watching Ike deal with the press, I don't think he needs a public relations adviser. He is tops." Butcher added that Eisenhower was so charming and affable with the press that "no one but a Sunday School teacher with a class of nice girls could have been as obliging as Ike."[4]

Next, Eisenhower tackled the state of British-Americans relations in the country. The British were sensitive to the presence of so many American soldiers in their nation, many of whom had little idea what the average British citizen had already endured in the war. Eisenhower had driven through the worst of the bombed sections of London, places where burned buildings rested alongside crater-filled streets. "Poor people, poor London,"[5] he muttered as he viewed the destruction and bodies, and vowed that the American soldier would treat every Briton with respect. He ordered a series of educational programs for his men that explained the war's history and the Londoners' experiences, described British customs, and took them on similar tours through the devastation.

When Eisenhower learned that one officer had drunkenly boasted that the Americans would teach the British how to fight, an irate Eisenhower vowed, "I'll make the son of a bitch swim back to America." In another incident, he ordered an officer reduced in rank and sent home after fighting with a British officer. When the British officer involved in the fight interceded for the American officer, claiming he had only called him a son-of-a-bitch, Eisenhower replied, "I am informed that he called you a *British* son of a bitch. That is quite different."[6]

Eisenhower consulted with top British officials to seek ways to smooth relations. In his headquarters, he paired an American officer with a British counterpart to avoid creating divisiveness. He needed unity as quickly as possible, not only for the immediate future but for the larger battles to come.

Eisenhower found a kindred soul in Winston Churchill, a factor that made his work easier throughout the war. Both individuals loved reading history, and Churchill thought it grand that Eisenhower had always wanted field commands. One evening General Walter Bedell Beetle Smith, Eisenhower's chief of staff, sat in mute wonder as Churchill and Eisenhower tried to top one another in historical knowledge. According to Smith, "Ike ran rings around the Prime Minister, throwing dates and events around like AA fire in a London blitz."[7]

But what most solidified the pair was their mutual hatred of Adolf Hitler—both burned with the desire to see the German dictator grovel in defeat.

⊬══⊣

The enormous workload took its toll on a weary Eisenhower, but he would labor as many hours as needed to defeat Hitler. "There is a lot to do here—sometimes there seems so much to do I can scarcely believe we can do it in time," he wrote Mamie on June 27. "But we've got to put it over, so we tear into the thing and never allow ourselves to think of failure." Later, he wrote his job required that he "be a bit of a diplomat—lawyer—promoter—sales-man—social hound—*liar* (at least to get out of social affairs)—mounte-bank—actor—Simon Legree—humanitarian—orator—and incidentally . . . a soldier! But I think I keep my feet on the ground and my brain fairly clear."[8]

Now that Eisenhower had risen to loftier command levels, he saw more clearly how important it was to possess a variety of talents. Eisenhower could no longer simply design and implement a plan for a platoon or company, as a lieutenant or a major could. He had to sell his ideas to dubious allies, fellow generals, and political leaders. In any war, the responsibilities multiply as a person steps up the command chain, and he or she must have multiple skills to meet those duties.

A few days later he wrote his mentor, Fox Conner, to inform him of the progress and of what lay ahead. "More and more in the last few days my mind has turned back to you and to the days when I was privileged to serve intimately under your wise counsel and leadership. I cannot tell you how much I would appreciate, at this moment, an opportunity for an hour's discussion with you on problems that constantly beset me."[9]

Conner would have been proud of the steps taken by his pupil, for he quickly won over not only the press, his soldiers, and most of his officers, but the British people. His humble Kansas origins resonated with the average citizen going about his daily life; he cut directly to the point in his speeches, rather than attempt to obfuscate matters, and his warm smile and good looks captivated women and made men want to work for him.

Londoners appreciated when he spoke bluntly of the challenges that lay ahead, yet with an optimism that made victory seem certain, and they responded to his "down-home" speaking style in which an important person was a "big shot" and gourmet food was "hifalutin."

The British became so fond of Eisenhower that taxi drivers waved and people shouted greetings when they spotted him. British Admiral Sir Andrew B. Cunningham typified the Londoners' reaction when he wrote, "I liked him at once. He struck me as being completely sincere, straightforward and very modest. In those early days I rather had the impression that he was not very sure of himself; but who could wonder at that? He was in supreme command of one of the greatest amphibious operations of all time, and was working in a strange country . . ." Cunningham added that "it was not long before one recognized him as the really great man he is— forceful, able, direct and far-seeing, with great charm of manner, and always with a rather naïve wonder at attaining the high position in which he found himself."[10]

+≈≈+

One of the main reasons why Roosevelt approved Marshall's selection of Eisenhower was the latter's ability to fashion workable teams wherever he served. His commands, such as with the tank corps and with the 15th Infantry, were known for their team spirit, and Roosevelt knew that the man in charge in London had to possess tact in abundance.

Eisenhower implemented an attitude of teamwork with the staff he fashioned at Grosvenor Square. He wanted "to see a big crowd of friends around here,"[11] and he quickly assembled a group that included his chief of staff, General Walter Bedell Beetle Smith, as well as his bodyguard and part-time driver Mickey McKeogh. He added naval aide Captain Harry Butcher to the team, a prewar journalist who knew the inner workings of the press, to handle the news agencies and to write an extensive diary of Eisenhower's tenure.

With frequent demands for his time, Eisenhower decided that he needed a man who could screen his visitors so he could focus on military matters. Chief of Staff Smith ably served in that capacity. He had no qualms telling anyone of any rank that he could not see Eisenhower or that his proposal would get nowhere. To Eisenhower's chagrin, Smith sometimes stepped over the line and offended people, and he often employed harsh words toward his staff, but those faults were worth it for the protection he provided Eisenhower. Eisenhower claimed that every leader needed an assistant to safeguard his time, fire incompetent officers, and carry out unpopular decisions, and for him, Smith was that man. They developed a mutual affection to the degree that Smith once blurted, "I love that man. The sun rises and sets on him for me."[12]

Reflective of Eisenhower's familial approach was his selection of living quarters in Great Britain. Within a week he had moved out of the exclusive Claridge Hotel, London's most expensive establishment, for a simple three-room suite at the Dorchester Hotel. He then arranged for an unobtrusive home in the country, called Telegraph Cottage, to serve as a sanctuary in which he could escape the pressures of command. Located along a golf course, the retreat offered time for Eisenhower to read his beloved Western novels, play bridge and golf, and recuperate from an exacting schedule.

"If anything saved him from a mental crack-up in those tense days it was Telegraph Cottage and the new life it provided," stated Kay Summersby, his driver during that time. Eisenhower banned military and political discussions at the cottage, for as he told Summersby, "After these long days at the office, worrying about operations which will involve the lives of hundreds of thousands, I don't want to worry when I get out here. That's the idea of this place. And that's the idea of my Westerns—when I read them I don't have to *think*."[13] After each sojourn in the country, Eisenhower returned with renewed energy and a fresh outlook.

Eisenhower was no different from the soldiers on the line, who benefited from occasional breaks from combat. His demands differed from theirs, but like the soldiers he nonetheless had a limit to his endurance. No matter what duties a person faces or in what war a soldier or officer may participate, quiet interludes are a requisite for consistent, efficient effort over a long period of time.

His first military challenge was where to mount the initial American action against Hitler. Though he hoped that the main cross-channel operation could occur as early as 1943, Roosevelt made it clear he expected a preliminary attack against Hitler sometime in 1942, partly to show to the Germans and to the American public that the American military was in the field, and partly to provide experience to the untested American military for when it did later cross the English Channel. The British, reeling from the recent loss of Tobruk in North Africa to Rommel, argued for an operation in that region. Eisenhower, who favored a more direct route to Germany, preferred to follow through with Operation Roundup, an attack along the European coastline.

As the British had been carrying the bulk of the fighting since 1939, their opinions carried a certain weight in this opening operation. Eisenhower received orders to plan for a large-scale amphibious assault against North Africa, called Operation Torch, while at the same time developing the proposed emergency cross-channel attack, Operation Sledgehammer, to assist the Russians in case they appeared to be in danger of collapsing in their struggle against the Germans. Eisenhower created a separate unit in the European Theater of Operations called Allied Force Headquarters (AFHQ), to plan the North African campaign. Before 1942 ended, the intricacies and political intrigues in North Africa combined with the spotty performances by American troops in their first tests against the Germans confounded Eisenhower as it also provided valuable experience in coalition warfare.

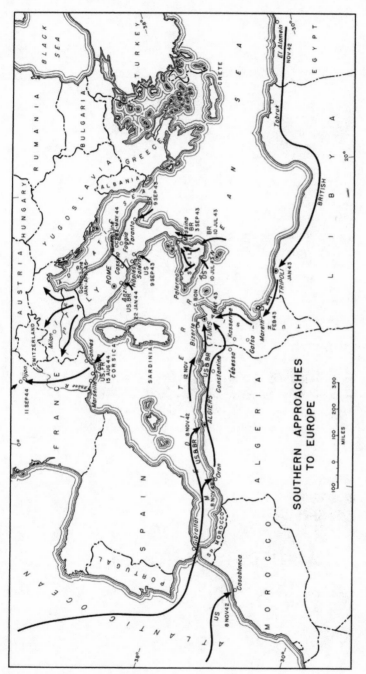

SOUTHERN APPROACHES
TO EUROPE

MILES
100   0   100   200   300

Introduction to War—the North African Campaign

CHAPTER 8

"We Sit on a Boiling Kettle!!"

EISENHOWER WAS ABOUT TO WADE INTO A POLITICAL LABYRINTH that made War Department intrigue appear amateurish. The Germans, who had overrun most of France in 1940, permitted the French to govern the southern portion of their country, which they labeled Vichy France after the city of that name, and to preside over part of the remnants of the French colonial empire in North Africa. Fearful of a harsh reaction from Berlin, some French officials in North Africa hesitated to implement any policy that might anger the Germans, while others, more closely aligned with the Free French forces who wanted the Germans out of France, quietly waited for the anticipated assault against Hitler. No one knew for certain the relative strength of the two French factions and whether any French official would assist or impede an Allied assault in North Africa.

Despite the numerous frustrations he faced, North Africa's dilemmas and problems became Eisenhower's classroom. Errors made in the sands and ridges of one continent prepared him for blustery beaches on another.

+≡≡≡+

Operation Torch called for a twofold thrust against German forces. While Eisenhower's American and British units landed at Casablanca, Algiers, and Oran—three port cities spread out over 1,200 miles of African coast—and advanced eastward, the British Eighth Army would push westward from Egypt against Rommel's vaunted Afrika Corps. If all went as planned, the two ends of the pincer would trap Rommel's men and drive the Germans from the continent. Eisenhower knew that failure in this first major operation would demoralize Allied forces and cost him his field command.

On September 14, 1942, Eisenhower explained to his senior American officers that only performance mattered. If they triumphed, he would do whatever he could to bolster their careers. If they failed, he intended to relieve them without hesitation.

Eisenhower wanted the soldiers to be thoroughly prepared. He reminded one group of officers that "Troops must be hard" and ordered continuous combat exercises and cross-country runs to keep the men trim and ready. "I cannot urge too strongly that emphasis be placed on individual and small unit training,"[1] he later stated. Eisenhower grasped, from his discussions with Fox Conner and from other examinations of military history, that the armies that are better prepared and trained triumph every time against those that are not.

After Hitler overran France, Marshal Henri Pétain established a new government in the town of Vichy; as premier he collaborated with the German occupiers in hopes of maintaining control over at least a portion of his country. As part of the arrangement, Vichy France continued to govern France's colonies in North Africa.

Eisenhower faced his first predicament—would the French in North Africa fight alongside their German occupiers, or could they be enticed to mount little or no opposition to the scheduled Allied landing? Two men appeared to hold the answer in their hands—French army General Henri

Giraud, who had strong support among many French leaders, and Admiral Jean Darlan, who had been named as Pétain's military successor. Some in the French military backed Giraud; others backed Darlan. Some detested the role Pétain played with Germany but felt bound to cooperate because Pétain represented the only legitimate French government. They would do what Pétain wished.

Eisenhower leaned toward working with Giraud, despite the fact that some French soldiers had pledged their loyalty to the Vichy government and were likely to remain steadfast. Eisenhower believed that Giraud commanded enough respect so that once the Allied forces landed in North Africa, he could unify the French there and convince them to help the Allies.

The Darlan group, duplicitously working with both sides to protect itself no matter what the war's outcome, insisted that Eisenhower work with the admiral. Eisenhower also faced pressure from Winston Churchill. The British leader wanted to prevent the French navy from falling into German hands and urged Eisenhower to, "Kiss Darlan's stern if you have to, but get the French navy."[2]

Uncertain as to which man to work with, Eisenhower nevertheless convinced Giraud to broadcast a message asking French units to cooperate with the Allies on the day of the landings. In return, Eisenhower would name him commander of French forces in North Africa.

A neophyte at such political intrigue, Eisenhower needed the French in his corner but lacked proper understanding of the volatile situation. French soldiers in Africa had already scorned French resistance leader Charles de Gaulle's overtures, citing loyalty to Pétain as their reason. It was unlikely they would thus acquiesce to any other French general.

Events moved quickly. On the afternoon of the November 8 landings Admiral Darlan distanced himself from Pétain and declared he was prepared to deal with the Allies. A frustrated Eisenhower now had two competitors for French command, each wanting to affirm his authority by assisting the operation. After half-joking that, "What I need around here is a damned good assassin!"[3] who could narrow his choices to one, Eisenhower allowed both French commanders to make broadcasts on November 9. In a turn of events that might appear comical were it not for the tragic implications, French soldiers in North Africa upheld their oaths to Pétain and promptly ignored the broadcasts. The situation deteriorated on November 10 when Pétain declared from Vichy that their appeals should be ignored. French soldiers fought alongside the German troops, forcing Eisenhower to face the challenge of Allied troops advancing against a military force that included an army that should have been an ally.

Hitler, of all people, unwittingly came to Eisenhower's aid the next day when he ordered German troops to occupy Vichy France and take over Pétain's government. With the marshal out of power, Darlan asserted that he now represented the legitimate government and that Eisenhower should deal solely with him. Eisenhower decided to work with Darlan. The move would satisfy Churchill, and he realized that Darlan and the French authorities knew the intricacies of North African tribal feuds and politics better than anyone in the Allied camp. But he underestimated the reaction that followed.

The deal's announcement on November 13 produced a torrent of criticism against Eisenhower, from the American press as well as from Roosevelt and Churchill. They accused Eisenhower of working with a Nazi collaborator who had implemented many anti-Jewish regulations, and they claimed that with this deal, Eisenhower had made a pact with a man who stood for everything against which the Allies were fighting.

Criticism came from other quarters as well. Soviet leader Josef Stalin worried that if his allies were willing negotiate with a fascist now, they might later join hands with Hitler against Russia. Resistance movements in other occupied nations wondered how much they could trust the Allies.

"Personally I've been under a great pressure, from all sides—and occasionally I wonder how I keep my good disposition," Eisenhower wrote to Mamie on November 27 of the perplexing days. "We sit on a boiling kettle!!"[4]

The besieged commander argued his case in a lengthy letter to his superiors. He saw no alternative to working with Darlan. Few soldiers listened to Giraud, and Roosevelt, put off by de Gaulle's arrogance, refused at this stage to work with the resistance leader. If he were to anticipate any stability in North Africa, Eisenhower needed at least a semblance of French authority to maintain control of civilian areas while he concentrated on military matters. Darlan would provide this.

When Marshall came to Eisenhower's defense, Roosevelt assented to the arrangement. To counter criticism of the Darlan deal, on November 26 George Marshall released casualty figures for the landings in North Africa. Although Allied planners forecast 18,000, due to unexpectedly soft opposition the totals had not exceeded 1,700. The difference, he explained, came from the Darlan agreement.

The ordeal disillusioned Eisenhower, who did not want to become one of those politicians he had long held in low regard. "I think sometimes that I am a cross between a one-time soldier, a pseudo-statesman, a jack-legged politician and a crooked diplomat,"[5] he wrote a friend. He was too kind to point out that his critics were hypocritical in damning him for working with Darlan at a time when the United States and Great Britain had allied themselves with the Soviet Union, one of the most oppressive regimes in the world.

At times like this, Eisenhower thought fondly of his days commanding the infantry, when he was free from political hassles and could make a difference in a soldier's life. He complained to Butcher, "If I could just get command of a battalion and get into a bullet battle, it would all be so simple."[6]

Despite his concerns, Eisenhower's experiences in North Africa prepared him for the more crucial, and bitter, times yet to come. This was his initiation, and like any such moment, errors would be made that could be corrected. As Marshall told Harry Butcher of Eisenhower, "He may think he has had troubles so far, including Darlan, but he will have so many before this war is over that Darlan will be nothing."[7]

⊢⇒⇐⊣

The military side of the North African campaign mirrored the political aspects as debates, mistakes, and criticism rolled right along with the tanks and the infantry. The first problem concerned Eisenhower's employment of a reserve force. Some commanders argued he should order the reserve into Bizerte, an important port in Tunisia, before the Germans were able to reinforce their troops by shifting units from nearby Sicily. On November 11, 1942, Eisenhower, feeling tentative as is often the case with a first-time command, ruled against the Bizerte operation. He felt the move sent Americans too far from their lines of supply. When Hitler quickly diverted aircraft and men from the fighting near Stalingrad to Bizerte, a barrage of criticism soon followed. Critics claimed Eisenhower had missed an opportunity to isolate the Germans already in North Africa from their supply lines and to advance Allied forces farther to the east. As a result, strongly reinforced Germans in Tunisia were able to slow the Allies' advance.

Supporters contended that Eisenhower reacted to the realities of the situation. Since Hitler maintained air and naval superiority near Bizerte, Eisenhower could be sending the reserves to be slaughtered. By allowing Hitler to reinforce Tunisia with troops that had been battling near Stalingrad, Eisenhower had come to Stalin's aid.

For similar reasons, Eisenhower rejected a request to dispatch a force to seize the island of Sardinia off Italy's western coast. If successful, the operation would hand Eisenhower airfields from which he could bomb Germans in North Africa, Sicily, and the Italian mainland, but Eisenhower believed the risks were too great.

Another commander—Patton comes to mind—would probably have made a more aggressive decision. With most of his previous work centering on staff assignments, however, Eisenhower was concerned about the risks his troops would have to take. This resulted in timidity rather than assertiveness.

His uncertainty showed in occasional outbursts, felt most often by staff members. "He suffered almost physically during January, February, and March . .,"[8] wrote Butcher. Morale at AFHQ sagged as Eisenhower learned the ropes.

He confided his frustrations to Mamie in a lengthy letter dated February 15, 1943. "Loneliness is the inescapable lot of a man holding such a job. Subordinates can advise, urge, help and pray—but only one man, in his own mind and heart, can decide 'Do we, or do we not?' The stakes are always highest, and the penalties are expressed in terms of loss of life or major or minor disasters to the nation. No man can always be right. So the struggle is to do one's best; to keep the brain and conscience clear; never to be swayed by unworthy motives or inconsequential reasons, but to strive to unearth the basic factors involved and then do one's duty." He added that while he had made progress, "I do not feel that I've 'arrived'—or that my major job is finished. I've just begun . . ."[9]

George Marshall sensed this mood in a January visit to Algiers. Eisenhower appeared so weary that Marshall ordered Ike's aide, Harry Butcher to make sure the general exercised and escaped the demands of his office, even if for only a few hours at a time. "It is your job in the war," he told Captain Butcher, "to make him take care of his health and keep that alert brain from overworking, particularly on things his staff can do for him."[10] Marshall later mentioned to Butcher that no matter what decisions Eisenhower made, his reputation rested on victory or defeat. Win in North Africa, and all the squabbles would be forgotten. Lose, and Eisenhower would be relegated to the backwaters of history.

At the January 1943 Casablanca Conference, Roosevelt and Churchill met to discuss the future strategy for the war. Eisenhower defended his decisions and stated that he had worked with Darlan because he knew that if the deal went wrong, Eisenhower could be blamed and be more easily replaced. According to presidential adviser Robert E. Sherwood, Eisenhower said that "generals could make mistakes and be fired but governments could not. He was entirely ready to take the rap for whatever went wrong."[11] An impressed Roosevelt and Churchill realized that Eisenhower's firm commitment to fashioning a unified Allied team meant more for the future than any relatively minor quarrels over troop placement or political deals. They even took the additional step of naming Eisenhower supreme commander for the follow-up assault against Sicily, with three British officers commanding the ground, naval, and air forces.

This incident proved to be a crucial moment for Eisenhower. Buttressed by the backing of his president and the British prime minister, he gained the confidence to assert his authority over men who had far more experience in warfare than he. This alone made Eisenhower a better-qualified leader and helped prepare him for the tasks to come. Almost as if the Joint Chiefs recognized the importance of this moment, two days later Eisenhower was promoted to a four-star general.

On February 14 Rommel launched his Afrika Corps against untested American forces at Sidi Bou Zid in Tunisia, with predictable results. Butcher labeled it "a severe licking" and concluded, "It's the worst walloping we have taken in this fight, and perhaps the stiffest setback of our ground forces in the war."[12]

Five days later, Rommel struck again, this time at a place named Kasserine Pass. Though the Americans suffered huge losses, subsequent counterattacks forced Rommel to at least pull back through a mountain pass.

Eisenhower urged his commander in the field, Major General Lloyd R. Fredendall, to more aggressively attack the long German supply lines and then to pursue the retreating Germans. When Fredendall adopted a more conservative approach and halted his troops, Eisenhower declined to step in with a firm order to move against Rommel. At a time when Eisenhower needed to be assertive, he allowed the pace to be determined by someone else and only suggested tactics that Fredendall should consider. Eisenhower could have issued clear-cut orders to Fredendall to ensure his wishes were followed, but he stopped short of doing so. This tendency to grant great autonomy to commanders in the field sometimes reaped dividends, as it later did with George Patton, but led to confusion and indecisiveness, as it did here and would later in the European campaign.

The appalling results at Sidi Bou Zid and Kasserine Pass showed Americans how vastly superior the Germans were. "The defeat has made all hands realize the toughness of the enemy and the need of battle experience for our own troops," wrote Butcher in his diary. "In fact, the correspondents have played up the so-called 'greenness' of American troops."[13] If they were to defeat the Germans, American soldiers and officers would have to improve dramatically.

Reports of lax discipline and poor training in Fredendall's command bothered Eisenhower, as did the information that Fredendall's headquarters stood one hundred miles from his front lines. "I'm sure you must have a better man than *that*,"[14] stated British general Sir Harold Alexander. Spurred by the advice, Eisenhower finally relieved Fredendall, a Marshall protégé.

Eisenhower sent him home and brought in George Patton, who speedily relieved incompetent officers, whipped the men into shape, and delivered two victories at Gafsa and El Guettar. Eisenhower had been slow to act on this matter, but once he did he moved with determination.

In formulating plans to push Rommel out of Tunisia, the British planned to advance General Alexander's 18th Army Group from the west and join with Montgomery's coming from the south, then drive Rommel to the sea. This, however, meant a supporting role only for the American forces. In April Eisenhower explained to Alexander that the American public would be so outraged over this slight that they would demand their troops be transferred to the Pacific. If they were not going to be employed in North Africa, they might as well be sent where they could do some good. Alexander relented and revised the plans.

Eisenhower used combat in Tunisia to hand another chance to an outfit that had performed poorly in earlier fighting at Kasserine, the 34th Infantry Division. Unlike Fredendall, who had committed a series of blunders over the course of time, Eisenhower saw promise in the 34th. He believed that if it participated in a successful assault, its morale would improve and the division would be valuable for the remainder of the war. Eisenhower ordered Omar Bradley to assign the division a key objective, a heavily defended hill. The 34th charged the Germans on April 30 and, despite heavy losses, seized the objective. The division became a stalwart in Eisenhower's roster for the rest of the war.

<hr/>

The entire American contingent learned valuable lessons in North Africa and progressed from their first action. In the first weeks of fighting in North Africa, *Time* magazine reported that while the British moved with precision, "the U.S. troops tentatively approached but never stormed the first of their heights."[15] By the end of the ten-month African campaign, however, American units had gained that hard, proficient edge that only combat can provide. They had learned the value of scouting and map reading, of defenses in depth, and of coordination between infantry and tanks. They had absorbed hard losses but picked up priceless experience along the way. Eisenhower discovered which officers he could trust to perform in combat and which he had to send home.

The end of the campaign in North Africa arrived in early May 1943. Bolstered by the presence of the aggressive General Patton and battle-hardened soldiers, the Americans linked with British forces in Tunisia and forced the Germans to the port city of Tunis.

Confined by the Mediterranean on one side and the Allies on the other, the Germans had nowhere to go. Fewer than 1,000, including Rommel, boarded German aircraft and escaped to Italy, but the bulk had to surrender. After savage combat, the Allies took the city on May 7.

By end of the fighting, Allied forces had secured Tunisia, driven the Germans out of North Africa, and captured 275,000 enemy soldiers. "The myth of his [Rommel] and Nazi invincibility had been completely destroyed," wrote Eisenhower. "It clearly signaled to friend and foe alike that the Allies were at last upon the march."[16]

Much work remained to be done, for despite the victory, American troops had shown they were far from ready for a cross-channel assault against the European mainland. Mistakes were inevitable, but both the supreme commander and his men started the process of remedying the errors. North Africa was Eisenhower's one chance to be wrong. He could not afford to repeat the same errors in 1944.

Fox Conner would have been proud of Eisenhower's most crucial contribution: Eisenhower showed that in its first major test against a well-trained foe, the Allied team could work together. He forged a coalition that, despite differences, overcame national loyalties. He had never led a squad or a company into combat, yet he succeeded in guiding troops from various nations to victory. He had been tentative along the way, but he adapted to the situation, learned from his mistakes, and became an improved commander.

When a junior officer errs in his first taste of combat, only his men and his immediate superior witness it. In his first combat experience, Eisenhower had Roosevelt, Churchill, Montgomery, and others looking over his shoulder. He prevailed in a situation that might have destroyed a lesser man.

Roosevelt wanted to award the Medal of Honor to Eisenhower for his work in Operation Torch, but Eisenhower declined. He felt the medal should be reserved for the soldier on the line, not the commander standing at headquarters miles behind.

Besides, Eisenhower knew his work was not complete. Too much combat remained before the medals were handed out, combat against an enemy that required total concentration and determination. When aides suggested he meet with a captured German general, Eisenhower dismissed the suggestion. This was war, not sports, and Germany was the enemy.

"For me World War II was far too personal a thing to entertain such feelings. Daily as it progressed there grew within me the conviction that as never before in a war between many nations the forces that stood for human good and men's rights were this time confronted by a completely evil conspiracy with which no compromise could be tolerated. Because only by the utter destruction of the Axis was a decent world possible, the war became for me a crusade in the traditional sense of that often misused word."[17]

Eisenhower expressed a sentiment that has not often been repeated since. Wars in the modern world frequently offer a less clearly delineated array of opponents—insurgent groups fighting for their nation, terrorist cells operating from multiple locations, religious sects battling for their beliefs. Eisenhower had the advantage of facing a clearly defined foe against whom he directed his full efforts.

With the North African campaign ended, Eisenhower turned his attention to the next stop on the way to Berlin—the island of Sicily.

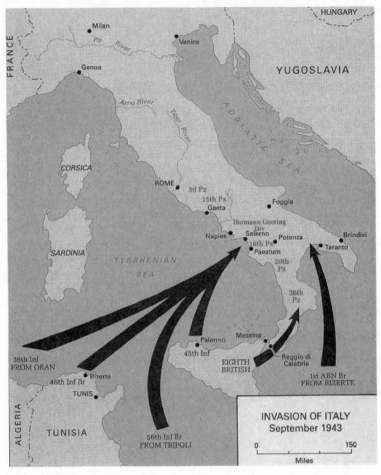

The Leap North to Italy

CHAPTER 9

"There Must Be a Fine Balance"

IN EVALUATING THE INACTIONS AT BIZERTE AND SARDINIA, GEORGE Marshall criticized Eisenhower for sometimes being too cautious in conducting campaigns. Eisenhower countered that he was not being conservative: He was trying to satisfy the conflicting demands of coalition warfare and was attempting to utilize the men and material available to him in the best possible way.

Eisenhower encountered the same issues that commanders past and present have faced when dealing with allies. For the good of the alliance, he had to check his natural inclination to favor his American cohorts. As commander, he could have easily diverted full support to George Patton, but that would only have caused problems down the road by offending Bernard Montgomery, a situation that could have possibly wrecked the coalition.

If Marshall or other critics needed evidence of his aggressiveness, Eisenhower used the June 1943 assault against Pantelleria, a Mediterranean island lying halfway between Tunisia and Sicily. Eisenhower coveted the airfield that rested on Pantelleria for its ability to support future operations in Italy, but most of his field commanders claimed the cost of grabbing one airfield would be too steep. The rocky island had few suitable landing sites, and no one could predict how strong a defense the 11,000 Italian troops would mount.

Eisenhower believed that if they arranged an intense preassault bombardment, Allied forces could land almost unopposed against an unnerved Italian garrison. To prove his point, four days before the scheduled attack, he boarded a British warship to reconnoiter the island. When the Italians responded with erratic fire from only two batteries, Eisenhower was convinced he was right.

On June 11 British troops approached Pantelleria from the sea. As Eisenhower predicted, the Italians surrendered without a fight, and by noon the island was firmly in Allied control. Eisenhower now possessed a valuable airfield from which to strike the Germans on Sicily, and more importantly, he gained a jolt of self-confidence for future operations.

"Today we took the Island of Pantelleria, as the papers will have told you by this evening," he wrote his wife. "I am particularly pleased because everything happened as I predicted it would."[1] He had suffered a tumultuous beginning in North Africa, but all it took to restore assurance was one smooth-running operation, even as small a one as Pantelleria.

The operation bolstered Eisenhower's confidence, in spite of British newspapers that heaped praise on the British commanders Montgomery and Alexander and overlooked his contributions. He wrote in his diary that, "They don't use the words 'initiative' and 'boldness' in talking of me, but often do in speaking of Alex and Monty." He thought that his insistence on using American troops in Tunisia and the outcome at Pantelleria more than proved his worth. "But it wearies me to be thought of as timid, when I've had to do things that were so risky as to be almost crazy. Oh hum."[2]

In May 1943 the Combined Chiefs of Staff met in Washington, D.C., to chart the path of the European fighting. They decided to stage the cross-channel assault in 1944, but left the details of operations in Sicily and the Italian mainland up to Eisenhower. Despite urgings from Churchill to leap right onto the Italian peninsula, Eisenhower selected Sicily as his next target. He believed that by planting Allied forces on Italian ground, the operation would lead to Italian dictator Benito Mussolini's downfall, cause the Germans to shift additional forces from the Russian front, and ease the pressure felt by the Russians.

After listening to arguments from both Montgomery, who promoted a full-scale attack against the southeastern corner of Sicily, and Patton, who wanted a more diversified approach including an assault closer to Messina, the major port on the northeastern tip, to cut off the Germans to the south, Eisenhower ruled in favor of the British commander. Montgomery's Eighth Army would land on the southeastern coast and advance along the eastern coast to Messina, while Patton's Seventh Army would come ashore to the west in support of Montgomery.

"This is what you get when your Commander-in-Chief ceases to be an American and becomes an Ally,"[3] lamented Patton. Eisenhower frequently found himself in a no-win situation. Should he adopt an idea promoted by American commanders, he was open to charges from the British that he acted only in behalf of his own country. Should he select a British concept, he would hear comments that he had meekly caved in to a foreign power. Eisenhower's single-mindedness helped him weather these charges, which worsened as the war continued.

Over the course of the past century commanders, from General Pershing in World War I to marine and army generals conducting operations in Iraq, have had to balance their own nation's interests with those of their allies. In turbulent times, Eisenhower found that what kept him on a level path was his devotion to a principle—in this case, maintaining the alliance—that transcended nationalism.

Allied troops landed on Sicily on July 10, when Patton's forces came ashore in the Gulf of Gela and Montgomery's near Syracuse. More than 500,000 Allied soldiers faced potentially strong resistance from 350,000 Italian and 30,000 German troops.

From the outset, turmoil marked the campaign. Eisenhower gave vast responsibility to his staff and an almost free hand to his two commanders, which resulted in chaos and a lack of clear direction. The stodgy, methodical Montgomery and the aggressive, impetuous Patton clashed from the start. Given freedom by their superior, they commanded their armies in their own fashion rather than act in accordance with the overall strategy. When Montgomery proceeded slowly against stiff German resistance, Patton expanded what should have been a supporting role into his own offensive thrust across the middle of Sicily to the north coast, and then east to Messina.

The Germans executed a remarkable defense, especially considering their Italian ally provided little help. After blocking Montgomery's Eighth Army along the coast, they pulled their forces back to the Italian mainland, thereby avoiding any trap the Allies hoped to spring. A swifter campaign, such as Patton had urged, marked by landings farther north along the coast toward Messina, might have trapped the bulk of the Germans forces and registered a more decisive win.

Eisenhower complained that Montgomery moved too slowly, but unwilling to openly interfere and possibly disrupt the alliance, he failed to issue clear orders that Montgomery should step up his pace and catch the Germans before they crossed to mainland Italy. Eisenhower wished Montgomery would move with some of Patton's speed and Patton would operate with some of Montgomery's attention to strategy, but at this stage he was not willing to assert his authority. Instead, he trusted his commanders to act to the best of their abilities. By the time Patton reached Messina on August 17, the Germans had already left for mainland Italy.

Eisenhower sensed that he had missed an opportunity here. He admitted to Mamie on August 18 that while he had achieved a victory, "I wish we could have taken a bit less time at the job . . ."[4] More than 50,000 Axis troops had escaped to the mainland, along with their weapons and supplies, thereby avoiding the annihilation hoped for by Eisenhower.

On August 17, the same day Patton occupied Messina, Eisenhower learned that his friend had committed a major blunder. While visiting hospitals during the two preceding weeks, Patton had met two soldiers suffering from battle fatigue, an illness Patton equated with cowardice. He abused the first soldier by calling him a coward and slapping him with his gloves, and in a separate incident twice struck the second soldier. Irate over what could become an embarrassing incident, Eisenhower dispatched men to investigate—one to Patton, one to the hospitals, and one to Patton's divisions to ascertain how soldiers viewed the affair.

After being briefed by the three investigators, Eisenhower concluded that he had to retain the valuable Patton, even if the American public demanded that he be relieved. He stated that the same qualities that caused Patton's eruption—impulsiveness, aggressiveness, emotion—were the attributes that made Patton such an outstanding leader of men, and that his contributions to victory would be indispensable. "He must be indifferent to fatigue and ruthless in demanding the last atom of physical energy," Eisenhower wrote after the war. "I felt that Patton should be saved for service in the great battles still facing us in Europe, yet I had to devise ways and means to minimize the harm that would certainly come from his impulsive action and to assure myself that it would not be repeated."[5]

Eisenhower wrote a lengthy, unofficial letter to Patton in which he reprimanded the general for his lapse, ordered him to apologize to the people involved, and warned that a repetition could cost him his command. A contrite Patton agreed to apologize. He penned a sincere apology to Eisenhower, claiming he had caused grief to a man he respected and promising to avoid such incidents in the future.

The episode seemed over until three respected journalists uncovered the details and asked to speak to the commander. Eisenhower convinced them that Patton had acted impulsively and that his removal would seriously impede the war effort. Eisenhower told them they could print their stories if they desired, but for the good of the army and of the country he asked them to refrain. In an action that showed the respect in which the press held Eisenhower, the trio assented.

The agreement lasted until November, when nationally prominent American newsman Drew Pearson aired the affair on his weekly radio program. A storm of criticism poured in, including some from powerful politicians, but Eisenhower refused to alter his decision. Patton would remain in command unless ordered out by Marshall.

In a letter to Marshall, Eisenhower defended his decision to retain Patton. He claimed that he had taken steps to prevent another such episode and believed that Patton would behave for one simple reason—glory. Eisenhower wrote that Patton "is so avid for recognition as a great military commander that he will ruthlessly suppress any habit of his own that will tend to jeopardize it."[6]

Eisenhower's spirited defense of Patton was one of his major contributions to the war. He knew controversy would always embroil Patton, but he recognized that with Patton in command, the war would end sooner than without him. Had Eisenhower caved in to the storm of protest and removed Patton, one is left to wonder how much slower the 1944 advance across France might have been.

It is appropriate that Eisenhower, who was always concerned for the welfare of his men, issued his most potent defense of Patton in a letter to the mother of a soldier serving in Europe. Mrs. June Jenkins Booth had written of her worry about her son serving under "such a cruel, profane, impatient officer" as Patton. The letter so moved Eisenhower that he wrote his response within one hour of receiving it on December 14, 1943.

"You are quite right in deploring acts such as his and in being incensed that they could occur in an American army. But in Sicily General Patton saved thousands of American lives. By his boldness, his speed, his drive, he won his part of the campaign by marching, more than he did by fighting. He drove himself and his men almost beyond human endurance, but because of this he minimized tragedy in American homes."[7]

Like commanders in other wars, Eisenhower faced the perplexing issue of what to do with an officer who abused his powers. Patton's ire might have been directed against prisoners of war or civilians, but in this case it was aimed at an unfortunate soldier who no longer had the ability to fight. Rather than succumb to heated criticism and emotion, Eisenhower judged the merits of the case and determined that Patton's actions, although detestable, did not warrant his removal. Eisenhower acted on what was best for the war effort, not on what might have been expedient. Eisenhower was then able to rely on his excellent relations with reporters to suppress the issue for at least a few months. One wonders what the outcome might have been had the press been less amenable to Eisenhower's request.

Eisenhower evaluated his own performance in Sicily and concluded that he had erred in two ways: an overestimation of enemy strength had caused him to be too conservative and, by landing too far from Messina, he had allowed the Germans to elude the Allies and live to fight another battle. He intended to possess a more accurate assessment of enemy capabilities and to act more aggressively in future operations.

The Combined Chiefs of Staff decided at the Quebec Conference in August 1943 that, while preparations for the assault against France from England would have priority, it made sense to send the forces in Sicily across to the Italian mainland. The troops and supplies were already in place, and possession of that country would provide valuable airfields from which to strike Germany. The thrust onto the Italian peninsula was a continuation of the fighting in Sicily—Allied forces laboring against superbly led Germans—with an unnerving dose of intrigue tossed in.

At first, Eisenhower must have thought he was back in North Africa, as he once again found himself in the midst of frustrating political maneuvering. Marshal Pietro Badoglio, who had replaced Benito Mussolini as head of the Italian government after the dictator had been deposed by the Fascist Grand Council, proposed on August 17 that as soon as the Allies landed on the mainland, his government would sign an armistice and declare war on Germany. The attractive offer contained a huge "if," however—Eisenhower had to guarantee that Allied forces would reach Rome before retreating German soldiers destroyed it.

Eisenhower would readily accept any offer that could potentially save Allied lives, but Roosevelt and Churchill worried about reaction at home from a deal with Hitler's ally. While Allied leaders debated the issue, Hitler sent additional forces to Italy, making Italian cooperation more imperative. When Allied units leaped across to the mainland from Sicily on September 3, Badoglio, fearing German reprisals against Rome and other cities, hesitated to announce an armistice, but Eisenhower reacted quickly and broadcast from his headquarters that the Italian government had surrendered. Presented with this preemptive move, the Italian government followed through with the armistice. Eisenhower had become more assertive.

As in Sicily, Allied units quickly bogged down in the face of stiff German resistance. Miserable conditions of rain, mud, and mountainous terrain aided the Germans, who forced the Allies to pay for every advance with heavy losses. Two months after the opening attack, Eisenhower wrote in his diary of the slow progress, "The country is unsuitable to the use of tanks and all the fighting has to be done by the infantry supported by artillery."[8] A costly war of attrition, similar to what American marines decades later faced in Afghanistan, forced the Allies to slug it out from mountain to mountain. In both cases, patience and a willingness to measure progress in small amounts became the overriding concerns.

⊱━━⊰

Toward the end of the year, Italy became a problem for another commander as the question of who would command the cross-channel assault into Normandy became pressing. The assumption had always been that George Marshall would guide this largest amphibious operation in history, code-named Overlord. Roosevelt said as much to Eisenhower in November 1943 when he explained that Marshall deserved a place in the history books and command at Normandy would guarantee it. "You and I know the name of the Chief of Staff in the Civil War," Roosevelt explained to Eisenhower, "but few Americans outside the professional services do." The president felt it would be a tremendous disservice to deny Marshall his rightful place in history, but indicated his hesitation by adding, "But it is dangerous to monkey with a winning team."[9]

Eisenhower longed to retain command for the Normandy assault, but understood Roosevelt's sentiments. He told the president he would happily serve wherever he was sent.

As the weeks passed, Roosevelt changed his mind. Marshall's expertise was simply too valuable for him to lose, so as much a disappointment as it must have been for Marshall, the president kept him in Washington. "I feel I could not sleep at night with you out of the country,"[10] Roosevelt consoled Marshall.

Since the American military would play the major role in the European campaign, it made sense that an American would be the commander, and Eisenhower was the obvious choice. His ability to mold a unified Allied team would be sorely needed in Europe.

"Eisenhower is the best politician among the military men," said the master of politics, Franklin Roosevelt, when asked by his son James why he had selected Eisenhower. "He is a natural leader who can convince other men to follow him, and this is what we need in his position more than any other quality."[11]

On December 7, 1943, two years after Pearl Harbor threw the nation into war, Roosevelt met Eisenhower in North Africa and said, "Well, Ike, you are going to command Overlord." A surprised Eisenhower checked his exuberance over the news and replied, "Mr. President, I realize such an appointment involved difficult decisions. I hope you will not be disappointed."[12]

Eisenhower was more than up to the task. He had developed skills in the succession of dreary army posts that had marked his early career and the larger campaigns in North Africa and Italy. His classroom had not been at West Point, but in postings with great men such as Fox Conner, George Patton, and Douglas MacArthur, and in the field with the 15th Infantry and the Third Army. He may not have exhibited the bravado and flair of Patton or the flowery oratory of MacArthur, but he possessed talents of his own that made him a capable leader—determination, fairness, and thoroughness.

On December 10, 1942, he wrote in his diary, as if referring to Patton, "The flashy, publicity-seeking type of adventurer can grab the headlines and be a hero in the eyes of the public, but he simply can't deliver the goods in high command." He followed with a comment seemingly aimed at Montgomery. "On the other hand, the slow, methodical, ritualistic person is absolutely valueless in a key position."

Eisenhower concluded that rather than relying on one style over the other, "There must be a fine balance—that is exceedingly difficult to find.

In addition to the above, a person in such a position must have an inexhaustible fund of nervous energy. He is called upon day and night to absorb the disappointments, the discouragements, and the doubts of his subordinates and to force them on to accomplishments, which they regard as impossible."[13]

In the years leading up to that moment, Eisenhower had frequently found himself trying to locate the fine balance between conflicting views, most often expressed with passion by Patton and Montgomery. Now, at last, he was ready.

The Eisenhower family in 1902. From left to right in the front row are David, Milton, and Ida; behind them stand the other five Eisenhower boys, Dwight, Edgar, Earl, Arthur, and Roy.

A sixteen-year-old Eisenhower (front center) enjoys a camping trip along the Smokey Hill River during the summer of 1907.

Eisenhower kicking a football at West Point in 1912.

Mamie and Dwight Eisenhower, holding toddler Icky, in 1918 outside their quarters near Gettysburg.

Eisenhower standing beside a tank at Camp Meade, Maryland, in 1919.

Colonel Eisenhower (right) sits with Harvey Firestone Jr. and Major Sereno Brett (left) at the Firestone Homestead in Columbiana, Ohio, during a rest halt in the 1919 cross-country expedition.

At the Firestone Homestead, Columbiana, Ohio
Sunday, July 13, 1919, a Rest Halt

Major Brett   Colonel Eisenhower
        Harvey Firestone, Jr.

70-520-3 E

(left) *Douglas MacArthur (center) with aides Eisenhower (right) and T.J. Davis at the Malacanang Palace, Philippines, in 1935.*

(below) *Eisenhower meets the press shortly after assuming command of the U.S. army's European Theater of Operations in London in June 1942.*

(left) *Generals Eisenhower and George C. Marshall in Algiers, June 1943.*

(below) *Eisenhower and Winston Churchill in northern France, shortly after the June 6, 1944, Normandy landings.*

(above) *The night of June 5, 1944, Eisenhower visited the paratroopers about to fly across the English Channel to begin the D-Day assault at Normandy. Eisenhower spent as much time as possible with the men he sent into battle.*

(left) *General Eisenhower presents an award for bravery to Corporal Stanley Appleby, Clarksville, New York (member of the US 1st Division). General Omar Bradley, far left, watches the ceremony.*

Eisenhower views the gruesome results of Nazi atrocities at the Ohrdruf Nord Concentration Camp. Such sights sickened his friend General George Patton.

At his headquarters in Reims, France, on May 7, 1945, Eisenhower holds the pens used to sign the German surrender document.

(above) *General Eisenhower waves to a jubilant crowd at the victory parade in New York City on June 19, 1945.*

(left) *President Eisenhower and Mamie on the White House steps, May 27, 1954.*

Supreme Commander

CHAPTER 10

"There Can Be No Thought of Failure"

GEORGE C. MARSHALL ORDERED EISENHOWER HOME FOR A BRIEF vacation before the rigorous demands of Operation Overlord took all his time and concentration. He spent much of the two-week vacation at the War Department, but did break away for a family reunion in Kansas. His mother and brothers immediately spotted a difference in Eisenhower. The affable grin was still evident, but he walked with new maturity, confidence, and determination. He appeared eager to return to his job, as if he felt the mission calling him.

"Looking at Ike now, you can't help but feel a little sorry for his enemies," his brother Arthur said at the time.[1]

Eisenhower flew to London in the middle of January 1944 to establish the Supreme Headquarters, Allied Expeditionary Force, SHAEF. Like his arrangement in North Africa, every British section chief had an American assistant and vice versa. In many ways, his work unfolded more smoothly this time, mainly because everyone, including him now, had experience in directing and supplying large armies. As he stated in his memoirs, "by comparison with the similar job of a year and a half earlier, order had replaced disorder and certainty and confidence had replaced fear and doubt."[2]

He also noticed that officers and staff seemed to labor with more focus, as they faced the largest amphibious operation in history that would determine the war's outcome. A February stag party thrown by the British officers who served under Eisenhower was evidence of the greater harmony that existed in London before the assault. The group presented Eisenhower with an elegant silver tray bearing all their signatures. First Sea Lord and British chief of naval staff, Admiral Sir Andrew B. Cunningham told the crowd he had first had his doubts abut Eisenhower when he took command in North Africa, but "It was not long before we discovered that our Commander was a man of outstanding integrity, transparent honesty and frank almost to an embarrassing degree."[3] He lauded the efforts Eisenhower made to mold a smooth-running Allied machine.

Nevertheless, Eisenhower still faced a series of problems that taxed his experience. The team assembled for the cross-channel assault had only begun its work. The attack's location and timing was set—Normandy, shortly after May 1. Sturdier German defenses bristled everywhere else along the Atlantic wall, particularly toward the north at Pas de Calais, the other logical spot to mount an invasion, which jutted closer to the British Isles than any other part of France. Mounting the operation in spring would give the Allies at least four months of decent weather before winter could hamper their operations. Furthermore, the only combination of moon and tidal conditions that would allow for a smooth landing occurred between early May and mid-June.

Having learned from his prior invasions of North Africa and Italy, Eisenhower took keen interest in the selection of division commanders for the crucial battle. He believed that these men would influence the battle more than other senior officers because the division was the largest military unit where an officer still made a difference. He was more visible and in touch with the men he commanded than a corps commander could ever hope to be. Soldiers could not identify with a corps or army, but to a man, they took pride in belonging to a certain division. Consequently, Eisenhower brought in officers who he either knew personally or came with strong recommendations from people he respected.

He then made sure the officers received publicity. Unlike MacArthur in the Pacific, where the only name issued in communiqués was his own, Eisenhower went out of his way to ensure his commanders received publicity back home. He asked reporters to write stories about different generals and colonels rather than only about him. By sharing the spotlight, he made division commanders feel more a part of the unit and created a more effective team.

Eisenhower did not let friendship shield incompetents, though. To safeguard the operation's secrecy, Eisenhower issued strict regulations forbidding any officer from talking about what he knew. In April Major General Henry J. Miller, one of Eisenhower's West Point classmates, mentioned a few details to partygoers after a night of heavy drinking. Eisenhower immediately reduced the man in rank and sent him back to the States. "Sometimes I get so angry at the occurrence of such needless and additional hazards that I could cheerfully shoot the offender myself,"[4] he wrote Marshall.

A dearth of landing craft plagued Eisenhower. To adequately land five divisions in May, he required almost three hundred more landing craft than he possessed in January. He pushed back the assault's date by one month, until June, to give more time for American factories to produce another hundred boats, then persuaded Marshall to postpone Anvil, a scheduled invasion of southern France, so he could use the landing craft earmarked for it.

Eisenhower finally had the boats he needed, although he had to beg and barter to scrape up the additional numbers. Winston Churchill grumbled that "the destinies of two great empires . . . seem to be tied up in some Goddamned things called LSTs [landing ship, tanks]."[5]

At a time of feverish activity, Eisenhower both exuded confidence and banned any pessimistic attitude. He knew the consequences for the war—success in Normandy would place the Allies on a path ending in Berlin, while failure would set the war's timetable back months, if not years. "This operation is being planned as a success," he admonished his staff as the weeks wound closer to June. "There can be no thought of failure. For I assure you there is no possibility of failure."[6] General Omar Bradley stated that Eisenhower's optimism so affected headquarters that even the most skeptical officer believed the operation would triumph.

One of Eisenhower's biggest concerns was Churchill. With the appalling losses suffered by British youth in the trenches of World War I and at the beaches of Gallipoli, the British leader feared another severe bloodletting in Normandy. He pestered Eisenhower about the assault force being too weak to wrench a beachhead from the Germans, and told the supreme commander, "When I think of the beaches of Normandy choked with the flower of American and British youth, and when, in my mind's eye, I see the tides running red with their blood, I have my doubts . . . I have my doubts."[7] Eisenhower reassured Churchill that every possible resource had been assembled for the attack and that the Allies would enjoy a victory.

One reason for Eisenhower's optimism rested with the volatile George Patton. He had rescued the impetuous officer's career after the slapping incident precisely because Patton's aggressive command style would be vital in fields and valleys of France and Germany. Once the armies broke out of Normandy, Patton's armored divisions could quickly rumble across the French countryside toward the German border. But Patton first had to make it to D-Day without committing another blunder.

On April 25 Patton again appeared in the headlines when, in a speech to a women's club England, he asserted it was the destiny of the United States and Great Britain to rule the world. The Soviet Union immediately protested this insult, and some American commentators called for Patton's dismissal.

"I'm just about fed up," Eisenhower bellowed to Bradley. "If I have to apologize publicly for George once more, I'm going to have to let him go, valuable as he is. I'm getting sick and tired of having to protect him. Life's much too short to put up with any more of it."[8] Eisenhower explained to

Bradley his disappointment that Patton had gone back on his word to behave after the slapping incident, and wondered if he had either the power or capability to save his hide.

Eisenhower waited for a signal from Marshall before making his decision. Marshall, who also wanted to retain the gifted commander who was clearly essential to winning the war, cabled that the decision regarding Patton was entirely in Eisenhower's hands.

Eisenhower called Patton to his headquarters, where a contrite Patton again promised to improve his behavior. Eisenhower came close to replacing him but could not risk losing such an important asset only months before the cross-channel operation. He glared at Patton and growled, "You owe us some victories; pay off and the world will deem me a wise man."[9] A grateful Patton vowed that Eisenhower would not regret his decision.

As frustrating and perplexing as Patton was, Eisenhower focused on one overriding factor—the man helped win battles. This alone enabled Eisenhower to suppress his anger and retain his friend, not because he was his friend but because his presence in the field made victory more likely. With that as his criterion, he handed Patton more autonomy than other officers might have had.

Eisenhower enjoyed success because he focused on the larger picture. If he wanted to benefit from Patton's abilities, he would have to suffer the controversies. A narrow approach might have meant a 1944 campaign in France without the inspirational, though frustrating, tank commander. Eisenhower was not prepared to face that situation.

While Patton controlled events on a battlefield, he could not control his mouth or emotions. Patton grabbed headlines and registered wins, but Eisenhower's steady hand and calm leadership made him a more complete command package.

<hr />

Whenever he required a break from the pressures of his job, Eisenhower found peace with the soldiers. Because he so cared about their welfare, a mutual understanding flourished between Eisenhower and the foot soldier that rarely existed between the general and other senior commanders. The foot soldiers were the men who executed his commands; they were the point of his sword. As such, they were the ones who died. Eisenhower diverted whatever precious hours he could from field marshals and prime ministers so he could mingle with the men who most felt the effects of his orders.

Eisenhower recognized the impact his orders carried—not just for the soldier, but for the man's family and friends as well. Many commanders send "units" and "divisions" into battle; Eisenhower sent "young boys" and "men." He personalized the war, and in doing so, he pondered the consequences longer than most.

An April 16, 1944, letter to Mamie illustrates his feelings on the matter. "How I wish this cruel business of war could be completed quickly." He added, "it is a terribly sad business to total up the casualties each day— even in an air war—and to realize how many youngsters are gone forever. A man must develop a veneer of callousness that lets him consider such things dispassionately; but he can never escape a recognition of the fact that back home the news brings anguish and suffering to families all over the country . . . War demands real toughness of fiber—not only in the soldiers that must endure, but in the homes that must sacrifice their best."[10] He undoubtedly had Icky in mind when writing these thoughts.

On a return visit to Normandy in 1964, he told newsman Walter Cronkite that the first thought that came to mind at revisiting Normandy was not the horrible weather that plagued the operation, not the infighting between Montgomery and Patton, not the immensity of the assault, but the families of those who died. He thought of their sacrifices, of never again seeing their sons or husbands or brothers, of not having grandchildren who might have been born.

As a result of this concern for the soldiers and their families, Eisenhower wanted to see as many men as possible before the attack. From February 1 to June 1, he visited 26 divisions, 24 airfields, 5 ships, and numerous supply depots and hospitals—a rate of about 5 or 6 a week. Instead of arranging the men by unit and delivering one speech to all, he preferred walking about the area, chatting informally with groups of a few at a time.

"Soldiers like to see the men who are directing operations," he wrote in his memoirs, "they properly resent any indication of neglect or indifference to them on the part of their commanders and invariably interpret a visit, even a brief one, as evidence of the commander's concern for them. Diffidence or modesty must never blind the commander to his duty of showing himself to his men, of speaking to them, of mingling with them to the extent of physical limitations. It pays big dividends in terms of morale, and morale, given rough equality in other things, is supreme on the battlefield."[11]

He received as much support from the men as he provided them, for their enthusiastic greetings and cheerful demeanors reassured him that his decisions, actions that had a direct bearing on whether they lived or died, were accepted. "When they called me Uncle Ike or . . . just plain Ike," he later confided to poet Carl Sandburg, "I knew everything was going well."[12]

He wrote to Marshall on May 21 that he liked what he saw in his visits. "There is no question at all as to the readiness of the troops. They are well trained, fit and impatient to get the job started and completed." He added that "At every stop I found morale and general readiness at the highest pitch."[13]

In the spring of 1944 he addressed the graduating class of the famed British military school at Sandhurst, an institution that had long produced some of Great Britain's finest officers. Instead of strategy or tactics, he spoke to them of the men they would command. He reminded the officers to consider them as family and to always take care of their men's needs before their own.

⊶⊷

The visits to his men bolstered Eisenhower and prepared him to face the problems and decisions that arose as the invasion drew near. Three problems in particular demanded his attention in the weeks leading to the assault—control of the air units, delays, and the weather.

The first problem involved the questions of which commander was to control the air forces in the Normandy assault and how the air units were to be employed. American officer Lieutenant General Carl A. Spaatz and British commander Air Chief Marshal Sir Arthur Harris argued that they should direct air operations for their respective air forces without interference, and that the main effort should be in the skies over Germany proper. Eisenhower countered that if Operation Overlord was to succeed, he required every possible military resource to be brought to bear in Normandy, particularly against the French transportation system, rather than Germany, and that he had to have control over their movements.

Though it was difficult for Eisenhower, he stood firm in the face of stiff opposition by powerful officers. On March 6 Patton visited Eisenhower's headquarters and listened as Eisenhower argued by telephone with Air Chief Marshal Sir Arthur W. Tedder, the deputy supreme allied commander. "I am tired of dealing with a lot of prima donnas," Eisenhower barked. "By God, you tell that bunch that if they can't get together and stop quarreling like children, I will tell the Prime Minister to get someone else to run this damn war. I'll quit."[14] Marshall sided with Eisenhower and handed him control of the air force for the duration of the Normandy campaign, but a second issue soon arose.

Churchill and the British War Cabinet feared that widespread bombing of the French railway system and road network would cause vast casualties—as many as 80,000 dead—among the French population at a time when the Allies needed their cooperation. Eisenhower answered that only a thorough bombing of the railroads could impede German efforts to rush reinforcements to the landings, and he doubted that an air offensive would produce anything close to 80,000 civilian deaths.

While the debate swelled, Beetle Smith, Eisenhower's chief of staff, astutely contacted de Gaulle's representative in London, Major General Pierre Joseph Koenig, to ascertain his opinion. After all, his countrymen stood to lose the most. "This is war," Koenig replied without hesitation, "and it must be expected that people will be killed. We would take the anticipated loss to be rid of the Germans."[15]

Any military mission carries with it the possibility for collateral damage, including the deaths of innocent people. Eisenhower weighed the estimation of French casualties against the benefits the bombing would have for the success of D-Day and concluded that any casualties caused by the bombings would be more than offset by the advantages gained for the Normandy assault. The choice could not have been easy for him, but he did exactly what a commander is supposed to do in such a circumstance—he made the difficult decision.

When Eisenhower repeated to Churchill his threat to resign, the British leader relented and debate ended. Eisenhower later claimed this insistence on targeting the French railway system was one of his greatest contributions to the war effort, as it so badly retarded any German effort to reinforce their troops at the beaches. After the war, when interrogated, German generals agreed that the preinvasion air campaign hamstrung their ability to move reinforcements.

+≻━≺+

With preparations for the June 6 attack well underway, Eisenhower held a May 15 meeting of all his senior commanders at the prestigious St. Paul's School, where Montgomery had been a student. With Winston Churchill and King George VI in attendance, Eisenhower asked each officer to explain the role of his forces in the invasion and to air any questions he might have. "I consider it to be the duty of anyone who sees a flaw in the plan not to hesitate to say so. I have no sympathy with anyone, whatever his station, who will not brook criticism. We are here to get the best possible results." Eisenhower wanted everyone committed to the same plan before they left the room.

After each commander spoke, Churchill delivered a ringing speech encouraging the men in the coming endeavor. Eisenhower then closed the meeting with a joke. "A few minutes from now, Hitler will have missed his last chance to wipe out the entire leadership of this operation with a single, well-placed bomb!" After letting the laughter subside, he turned to his main point. "I want everyone here to see himself as being part of a staff college for the future. This will be a college in which there is neither Army or Navy or Air Force; not British or American; but a college consisting of nothing but fighting men who are there to learn, and to teach others, the art of future wars."[16]

His prescient words carried meaning for future wars. Because of Eisenhower's efforts in building a coalition out of diverse interests, commanders in the Korean conflict and in Iraq had an example to follow. Eisenhower's actions could help guide them in their equally daunting tasks.

Two weeks later, on May 30, another crisis loomed when British Air Chief Marshal Leigh-Mallory informed Eisenhower that the Germans had reinforced the region where Allied airborne forces intended to land. Leigh-Mallory feared that if they went ahead with the operation, the units would leap into a slaughter.

Eisenhower faced a major decision with the assault only one week away: Should he postpone the airborne assault and, with it, the entire operation, or should he risk disaster and maintain the schedule? In an action eerily similar to what General George Meade had done that night at Gettysburg, he headed off to be alone and ponder his next move. He carefully reexamined each facet of the attack and grappled with the notion that if he rejected Leigh-Mallory's advice and the attack failed, "then I would carry to my grave the unbearable burden of a conscience justly accusing me of the stupid, blind sacrifice of thousands of the flower of our youth."[17]

After weighing the alternatives, Eisenhower decided to continue the operation as planned. He faced similar dire predictions in Sicily and Italy without result, and he could not allow what amounted to an educated guess by Leigh-Mallory to derail the entire cross-channel attack.

The anxieties affected Eisenhower, who chain-smoked four packs of cigarettes a day. He wrote in his diary on June 3, "Probably no one who does not have to bear the specific and direct responsibility of making the final decision as to what to do can understand the intensity of these burdens."[18]

+=====+

On June 3 he also wrote in his diary about what became his biggest concern in the days leading up to the assault—the weather. Eisenhower controlled every detail of a complex plan but he could not control Mother Nature. Men could be in place, the machines of war could be oiled and ready, but all could go for naught depending on the whims of nature. He wrote in his diary that "the uncertainty of the weather is such that we could never anticipate really perfect weather coincident with proper tidal conditions, that we must go unless there is a real and very serious deterioration in the weather."[19]

Unfortunately, Eisenhower faced just such a situation, as winds and rain buffeted the English coast and churned the waters of the English Channel. He met with his Meteorologic Committee twice each day—in the early morning and again in the evening—to receive updates about the crisis, which appeared serious enough to warrant delays. On the morning of Sunday, June 4, with the weather worsening, he postponed D-Day twenty-four hours. The intended June 5 attack would, if the weather somehow improved, now occur on June 6.

At the June 4 evening session, meteorologists informed Eisenhower that a break in the weather might enable the attack to proceed on June 6, but that overcast skies would be a problem, especially for the airborne units. If Eisenhower canceled the June 6 date, he would have to wait for at least two more weeks before favorable tidal and lunar conditions existed.

As Eisenhower paced the room, he halted before each of his senior commanders, stared directly into their eyes, and asked their opinions. Beetle Smith and Bernard Montgomery favored going ahead, while Sir Arthur Tedder cautioned the operation would be a huge risk. Eisenhower said he leaned toward proceeding but would make the final decision after the weather report at the next morning's meeting.

Early in the morning of June 5, Eisenhower again assembled his commanders. They reviewed the plans and weather situation one last time, then everyone quieted and waited for the supreme commander to issue his verdict.

Beetle Smith observed Eisenhower as he struggled with such a monumental decision and was relieved he did not have to fill those shoes. "I never realized before the loneliness and isolation of a commander at a time when such a momentous decision has to be taken, with full knowledge that failure or success rests on his judgment alone."

Eisenhower sat for a time, deep in thought, then suddenly looked up and declared, "Well, we'll go!"[20]

With those three words, Eisenhower started the war's largest amphibious operation. The commanders rushed to waiting vehicles to join their forces, while Eisenhower remained at headquarters and tried not to dwell on the men he was sending to their deaths. Now that the decision to go had been made, he was powerless over the immediate course of events. The outcome now rested in the hands of the British, Canadian, and American soldiers, and to luck. He could do nothing but wait.

Eisenhower played a game called Hounds and Fox with an aide, then earned a draw in checkers in a heated match with his naval aide, Captain Harry Butcher. With a cigarette in one hand and a cup of coffee in the other, he idled the hours, wishing he knew what was happening above and across the channel. Few could know what he faced. Certainly General Meade had known. Definitely William the Conqueror had known, who in 1066 had also crossed the channel. The seas had been unexpectedly calm for the North African landings, and horrible weather over Sicily had cleared at the final moment. Would Eisenhower's good fortune with the weather from previous operations carry over to Normandy?

Winston Churchill now provided words of comfort to Eisenhower. He claimed that if by winter Eisenhower had 36 divisions on the continent and had secured the Normandy and Brittany regions, he would "proclaim this operation to the world as one of the most successful of the war. And if, in addition to this, you have secured the port of Le Havre and freed beautiful Paris from the hands of the enemy, I will assert the victory to be the greatest of modern times."[21] Eisenhower welcomed these words, then assured the prime minister that by the winter of 1944, the Allied army would rest on the German border.

Eisenhower had no way of knowing how accurate his declaration would be. The only thing certain was that he stood at the brink of the cross-channel operation that Fox Conner had predicted in the 1920s. He, the student, had to wonder what Conner, the teacher, would think of his protégé. "I hope to God I know what I'm doing,"[22] he muttered to his staff.

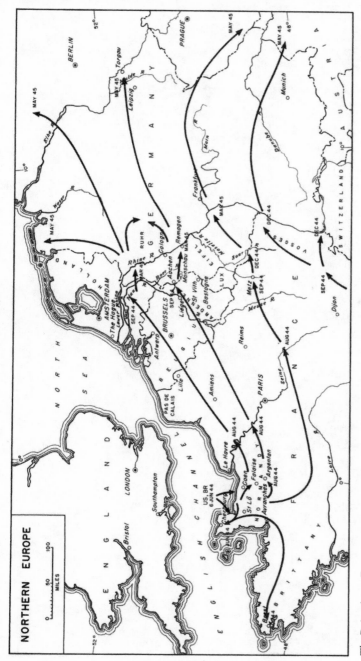

The Drive Across Europe

CHAPTER 11

✛≕≕✛

"The Great Crusade"

MORE THAN 4,000 ALLIED SHIPS, AIDED BY 3,500 HEAVY BOMBERS and 5,000 fighter planes, transported over 150,000 troops to Normandy's shores on June 6. Eisenhower hated the feeling that he could no longer affect the day's proceedings. All he could do was wait until he received word of the outcome. "Again I had to endure the interminable wait that always intervenes between the final decision of the high command and the earliest possible determination of success or failure in such ventures."[1]

His Order of the Day reflected an optimism that, while not misplaced, was also not wholly justified under the precarious circumstances. The weather, the strength of the German forces opposing them, cooperation of the French populace, the readiness of the Allied units, luck—all these had a bearing on whether the evening of June 6 would be marked with congratulations or with condolences. "Soldiers, Sailors and Airmen of the Allied Expeditionary Forces!" the Order of the Day began. "You are about to embark upon the Great Crusade, toward which we have striven these many months. The eyes of the world are upon you. The hopes and prayers of liberty-loving people everywhere march with you."[2]

Eisenhower composed a second message, one he prayed he would never had to broadcast—an announcement to be used in case the operation failed and he had to withdraw his forces. The words directly contrasted with his Order of the Day and must have been painful to write, but Eisenhower wanted to be prepared for any contingency. If the Germans repulsed the invasion, he intended to take full blame for the debacle. "My decision to attack at this time and place was based upon the best information available. The troops, the air and the Navy did all that Bravery [sic] and devotion to duty could do. If any blame or fault attaches to the attempt it is mine alone."[3] After writing it, Eisenhower carefully folded the announcement, placed it in his wallet, and headed off to eat.

⊷⊷⊷

As Eisenhower puffed his way through his daily four packs of cigarettes, information trickled in. First reports offered a glimmer of hope—the airborne units had not been slaughtered. Despite suffering heavy losses and troops being air-dropped miles from the objectives in the stiff winds, key positions had been secured or attacked. Troops landed against light opposition at four of the five invasion beaches, while a bitter battle raged at the fifth. His naval aide, Captain Harry Butcher, wrote that, "The landings have gone better than expected. Every outfit is ashore, but we have just had a report that Gee, Major General Gerow, with his V Corps, can't get off one of its beaches because of hostile mortar and artillery fire. This is Omaha Beach."[4]

Fortunately, it appeared the Germans had been successfully tricked into thinking the landings would occur to the northeast, at Pas de Calais. The German units stationed in that region remained in place and did not rush to Normandy. By evening of D-Day, 156,000 Allied soldiers, supported by tanks and artillery on the ground and a potent air screen above, established beachheads stretching along a thirty-mile-wide front. There had been ten thousand casualties, which was an alarming number, but half what planners anticipated.

Of course, not all went according to plan. Montgomery boasted that he would seize the French city of Caen by the end of D-Day, but the British general had been slow to push off the beaches. Eisenhower needed the terrain about Caen so he could construct airfields to support the breakout from the beaches and the drive across France toward Germany.

Allied forces poured off the beaches in the following days and seized enough ground that Eisenhower felt safe enough to cross over for a visit. On June 12, accompanied by a recently arrived General George Marshall and the chief of naval operations Admiral Ernest King, Eisenhower landed at Omaha Beach, which had been wrested from the Germans after a horrifying struggle. The commanders inspected a bridgehead that had pushed eight to twelve miles into the French countryside and stretched fifty miles wide.

Conditions appeared promising. On June 9 he wrote Mamie, "But all that can be done by human effort, intense devotion to duty, and courageous execution, all by thousands and thousands of individuals, will be done by this force. The soldiers, sailors, and airmen are indescribable in their élan, courage, determination and fortitude." After praising the efforts of his soldiers, a moved Eisenhower added, "They inspire me."[5]

After the initial advances, the Allied attack stalled all along the line. In the eastern end, Montgomery continued to struggle against the Germans defending Caen. By month's end he still had not taken the objective that he had claimed he would have in hand on June 6. To the west, American forces pushed inland from Omaha and Utah Beaches, but bogged down in the tortuous hedgerows that surrounded French fields and transformed pastoral farmlands into German bastions. Hidden by the thick bushes, German machine gun crews waited for American units to draw near, then decimated them with blistering fire. The stalemate along the Allied line resulted in a dangerous backup—forces and supplies waiting to come in from England had to remain across the channel until the Germans retreated. Eisenhower could not fuel a drive across France with essential men and weapons idling in England's harbors.

Some suggested that Eisenhower send a stern message to Montgomery about his slow pace and order him to move out from the beaches, but true to the command style he first exhibited in North Africa, Eisenhower refused. Montgomery had his orders and knew how important it was for him to advance, and Eisenhower hated to step in. He preferred to give his commanders in the field a measure of freedom rather than run the show from London, for he believed that approach produced greater benefits than if he forced a commander's hand. Throughout the remainder of the war, Eisenhower hesitated to issue overriding orders dictating a commander's course of action. He outlined the general picture and determined the goals, then allowed his commanders to fill in the details.

He had another reason for allowing his commanders freedom of execution. Recalling Fox Conner's words, Eisenhower knew how important it was to fashion a smooth-working Allied machine. He could not keep harmony among the Allies if his orders constantly irritated one commander or another, so he tried to be somewhat open in running the offensives. How would it look, for instance, if the American Eisenhower constantly badgered the British Montgomery, especially as the British people considered Montgomery a hero for his role in earlier battles in North Africa? He had an easier time with his American commanders, but even there, strong personalities, especially that of his tank friend, George Patton, made his life difficult.

Instead of direct orders, Eisenhower often relied on suggestions or on personal visits. If Eisenhower decided to fly in to a commander's headquarters, it usually was because he hoped the visit would prod the man into taking one choice of action rather than another. He might sit down and discuss tactics, but he rarely phrased his thoughts in the form of an order. His presence, not his words, was meant to convey his wishes. He believed that a commander who handed out frequent orders lost the respect of his subordinates and negated the abilities of the officers he hoped to influence. Eisenhower wanted his commanders to employ their knowledge and experience, not shelve them.

When he had earlier commanded infantry, Eisenhower made sure his men understood the precise reasons for his orders and what an operation entailed, but he believed he could not be as forceful with the temperamental Montgomery or the mercurial Patton. He had to keep the Allied attack going, so unless dire circumstances forced his hand, he preferred a loose command.

In handing greater freedom to subordinate commanders, Eisenhower may have guaranteed continued action along the front, but he also created a situation that critics could use against him and that strong-willed personalities could take advantage of. Some officers, especially Montgomery and Patton, misinterpreted Eisenhower's command style as a weakness they could exploit. Eisenhower's son John, recently graduated from West Point, accompanied his father during a June 15 visit to Montgomery's headquarters and observed how difficult it was for anyone to deal with the British commander. Montgomery acted as if unwanted visitors had approached his throne. "Monty did not seem to notice me or anyone else, almost including Ike,"[6] he wrote later.

On the other hand, Eisenhower received criticism from Patton for not being tougher on his British counterpart. Patton wrote in his diary on July 12 that, "Ike is bound hand and foot by the British and does not know it. Poor fool. We actually have no Supreme Commander—no one who can take hold and say that this shall be done and that shall not be done."[7] Patton conveniently glossed over the glaring fact that he detested it when Eisenhower interfered with his wishes.

Finally, on July 18, Montgomery's Second Army secured Caen. Montgomery failed to take advantage of the occasion by pushing beyond the city against the retreating Germans, as Eisenhower had suggested, and this angered him. Montgomery claimed he had to regroup and resupply his forces before moving on. Eisenhower's naval aide, Captain Butcher, recalled that when Eisenhower learned of Montgomery's pause, "Ike was mad. Monty always wants to wait to draw up his 'administrative tail.'"[8]

The seizure of Caen coincided with movement along the American side as well. General Omar Bradley hoped to drive his units through German lines, at which time Patton would veer west into Brittany. The operation, called Cobra, enjoyed swift success after commencing on July 25. Once the Americans shattered the German defense lines, they learned that the German left flank lay open. Instead of sending all of Patton's troops west into Brittany, Bradley ordered one corps to head west while the others took advantage of the opening and charged east. Patton's famous dash across France with his armored units had begun, thus fulfilling Patton's prediction years earlier that one day Patton would lead tanks in a battle commanded by Eisenhower.

On August 7, with Allied forces hammering huge holes in the German lines, Eisenhower established his forward headquarters in Normandy. General Bradley commanded the 12th Army Group on the southern end of the Allied advance, consisting of the First Army under General Courtney Hodges and Patton's Third Army, while Montgomery in the north led the 21st Army Group, consisting of the First Canadian Army and the Second British Army. The march to the German border was in motion.

Hitler had other plans, however. As Patton's forces split into two drives, a gap opened near the city of Mortain at the southern end of the Cotentin Peninsula. Hitler ordered a counterattack to push through Mortain and head toward Avranches at the peninsula's western coast. If successful, the move would sever the supply lines to the troops in Brittany and force the Allies to pull back toward the invasion beaches.

Hitler's field commander in the west, Field Marshal Gunther von Kluge, advised against the operation in favor of pulling back to the Seine River. A failure at Mortain would leave France wide open to an Allied drive that would not halt until the German border. Hitler ignored the suggestion and ordered the attack for August 7. "That decision, more than any other, was to cost the enemy the Battle for France,"[9] Bradley wrote after the war.

Allied intelligence learned of the German move ahead of time, so that when the German attack commenced, Eisenhower's forces were prepared. While designated units absorbed the initial thrust and held the Germans near Mortain, other American troops under Patton veered around the German left flank to the south. With Montgomery's British driving down from the north, the Germans would find themselves trapped between the Americans in the south and the British in the north. All Montgomery and Patton had to do was link up behind the German lines and von Kluge's invaders would be surrounded.

The German commander's fears materialized. The Allies had his men in a tight grip, with his only avenue of escape to the east in danger of being slammed shut. "To a staff officer," wrote Beetle Smith, "seeing it all in the red, blue, and black symbols on the map, it was almost unbelievable that the German High Command could have left the bulk of its forces in France be maneuvered into such a desperate situation."[10]

On August 9, facing stiff opposition from Allied air and ground forces, von Kluge halted his attack. Two days later the Germans began retreating, but by August 14 there was only a small gap between Patton's and Montgomery's lines.

In order to avoid the two armies from charging into each other, Bradley ordered the faster-moving Patton to halt at the town of Argentan, as stipulated by the plans. Patton argued he should move beyond the town and close the gap even sooner, but Bradley feared the Americans would run into the British and, in the confusion of the moment, the two forces would accidentally start firing at each other.

Patton heatedly objected to the order, claiming it would only permit more Germans to escape the encirclement. He contended that Montgomery moved too slowly, and every moment lost in shutting the door behind the enemy resulted in fewer men being trapped. He ordered his commanders to be ready to drive beyond Falaise and "drive the British back into the sea for another Dunkirk."[11]

To Patton's dismay, Bradley stuck to the original plan. Montgomery eventually joined with Patton, but in the interval as many as 40,000 German soldiers fled through the gap above Argentan, a number that garnered criticism for both Bradley and Eisenhower. However, this criticism loses sight of the fact that the Germans lost 75,000 men, almost all their supplies, and more importantly, the French countryside that had been conquered provided an open path to the German border for a commander with the flair for lightning-quick offensives. Patton was about to take center stage.

On another of his visits to the front, Eisenhower was struck by the death and devastation near Falaise. "The battlefield at Falaise was unquestionably one of the greatest 'killing grounds' of any of the war areas. Roads, highways, and fields were so choked with destroyed equipment and with dead men and animals that passage through the area was extremely difficult. Forty-eight hours after the closing of the gap I was conducted through it on foot, to encounter scenes that could be described only by Dante. It was literally possible to walk for hundreds of yards at a time, stepping on nothing but dead and decaying flesh."[12]

┼═══┼

With the victorious fighting near Mortain, Eisenhower had chased the Germans out of Normandy and had created an opportunity to drive them eastward out of France. Before pushing eastward, though, he had to resolve two nagging issues. The first involved the planned assault against southern France by the U.S. Seventh Army to seize the valuable port of Marseille. Eisenhower favored the operation so he could utilize the port facilities for the drive across France and to force the enemy to fight on a new front. He also needed additional American divisions to apply pressure on the Germans from the south of France while his forces broke out of Normandy and pushed across the middle and northern portions of the country.

Instead of the operation in southern France, Winston Churchill favored using the forces in Italy or in the Balkans to Italy's east. Eisenhower believed that Churchill's thinking was guided by postwar political considerations. The prime minister hoped to preclude the Soviet Union from gaining the upper hand in the region, and while Eisenhower had no objections to Churchill's ambitions, he argued that it was a dispute for Churchill to resolve with Roosevelt.

In an August 7 meeting with Eisenhower, Churchill pleaded his case for six hours, but Eisenhower would not be deflected from his strategy, even in the face of such a formidable debater as the prime minister. "Ike said no, continued saying no all afternoon, and ended saying no in every form of the English language at his command," Butcher recorded of the meeting. Eisenhower told Churchill that he had based his decision on "sound strategy," and that Anvil "would further extend the enemy." An unconvinced prime minister departed, leaving a "practically limp"[13] Eisenhower, who hoped President Roosevelt would step in on his behalf.

When the president agreed with Eisenhower, the attack into southern France unfolded as planned on August 15. Within two weeks the Allies seized Marseilles, handing a valuable port facility to Eisenhower, and had quickly advanced up the Rhone Valley against light opposition. The subsequent value of Marseille to bringing in supplies and reinforcements justified Eisenhower's advocacy of the operation.

The other problem concerned the city of Paris, long the cultural center of France. Eisenhower preferred to divert his troops around the city, drive on to Germany, and let the French handle their own problems, but French partisans in Paris forced his hand on August 19 when they seized control of the city and signed an armistice with the German commander. When French Resistance leader, Charles De Gaulle, then asked Eisenhower to send Allied units into the capital, Eisenhower, who did not want to risk offending the French, had little choice but to agree. He would now not only have to maintain an adequate flow of supplies to his soldiers fighting the Germans, but provision two million civilians in the French capital.

The unexpected development diverted trucks, manpower, and supplies at a time when Eisenhower dearly needed them at the front. Commanders in all wars face unplanned emergencies that sap the resources at their disposal, such as the American military officers faced later in Iraq, when they experienced a shortage of armored vehicles. Rather than allow the situation to bother him, Eisenhower handed the matter to his staff and turned to the main task at hand, which for him meant the defeat of Nazi Germany.

⊹═━═⊹

The political aspects of the war had long vexed Eisenhower. He was a military man on a military mission, and when the strain of politics became too pressing, he sought the company of his men at the front. The world was less complex to infantrymen who wanted to get the war over with and head home. The simplicity of that outlook appealed to Eisenhower.

The soldiers responded with unabashed affection for their supreme commander, for he had shown in many ways that he cared about them. He ordered that whatever rest and recreation facilities were made available to officers also had to be established for the enlisted men. Troops recalled fondly the time when Eisenhower learned that two high-ranking officers set up luxurious accommodations for officers in expensive villas.

He ordered the offenders out and stipulated that the locations be reserved instead for enlisted men.

Eisenhower emphasized the importance of taking care of the men under one's command to his son during John's June 1944 visit. Most likely recalling the time in the transport heading to Panama, when the pair of generals had kicked Mamie and him out of their quarters, Eisenhower admonished John about commanding his first platoon, "Go around and see every man, see that he gets into warm, dry clothing . . . that he gets a good hot meal and that his weapons are in tiptop shape. Shoes, socks and feet are of tremendous importance, and you should try to wear exactly the same kind of materials as your men do when in field training or in combat. By pursuing these methods you will not only have a splendidly trained platoon, but one that will follow you anywhere."[14]

His visits to the troops cheered them in other ways, for Eisenhower was not a commander who avoided the front lines. During a July trip, Eisenhower hopped into a jeep and, without realizing it, crossed into German-held territory. On July 4 he flew over the hedgerow country in a fighter, not to assert his courage but as "a gesture to our pursuit pilots who are doing yeoman work in attempting to find and plaster targets."[15] He feared that Patton's tanks and Montgomery's infantry would so dominate the headlines that the labor of the fighter pilots would pass unrecognized.

After a thorough victory at Falaise, Eisenhower sent the Allied forces east through France. Montgomery and his 21st Army Group headed along the northern approaches to Belgium, while Bradley's First and Third Army—the latter commanded by Patton—charged across the middle of France. During three weeks in August and September, as much as two hundred miles of France fell into Allied hands. An air of optimism swept through Allied headquarters.

"The defeat of the German armies is complete," Eisenhower wrote in his diary on September 5, "and the only thing now needed to realize the whole conception is speed."[16]

The Germans may have been falling back toward their borders, but Eisenhower still faced opposition from two Allied commanders who refused to yield ground. A series of encounters with Montgomery and Patton would push Eisenhower to the limits of his incredible patience.

CHAPTER 12

"A Jewel of Broad-Mindedness and Wisdom"

NOW THAT THE ALLIES HAD PUSHED INTO THE FRENCH COUNtryside, the question of how to advance toward and into Germany dominated Eisenhower's time. A strategy had been formulated before Operation Overlord began—the Allies would maintain two simultaneous drives along a broad front across France. General Bernard Montgomery would command the one in the north that would spread out across northern France, move through Belgium north of the Ardennes forest, and into the valuable Ruhr factory region in Germany.

As Montgomery shepherded his armies along this northern route, General Omar Bradley would lead American forces out of the Cotentin Peninsula, bypass Paris, move north of the Ardennes, and proceed into

Germany near Cologne south of the Ruhr. Once inside Germany, both vast armies would encircle the Ruhr before racing across the remainder of Germany. The two forces would provide mutual support for each other and keep the Germans guessing as to which, if any, route formed the main thrust. Until the Germans knew for certain, they would have to station troops all along the line rather than mass them against a single powerful attack at one location.

The plan stipulated that of the two drives, Montgomery's would receive priority whenever a question arose about tactics or supplies. Excellent port facilities existed for the Allies in his region, and the launching sites for Hitler's new V–1 rockets that had terrorized London were located there as well. Unless faced with such a quandary, however, Eisenhower would send men and material in equal measure along the line. He wanted to keep the Germans off balance, and would only veer from the strategy if an exceptional opportunity arose. Eisenhower possessed the manpower and supplies to maintain fighting all along the line, and in much the manner of Ulysses S. Grant, who adopted the same strategy in routing the Confederate forces in the Civil War, he would keep constant pressure on the enemy.

The plan worked to perfection in late August and early September. In mere days, Montgomery raced by those same World War I battlefields on which for weeks and months thirty years earlier soldiers had fought and died. American forces crossed the Seine River on August 27, and three days later Patton, having earlier been diverted south by Bradley, triumphantly led his troops across the Meuse River about 50 miles from the German border.

The unexpected progress led to a flurry of statements and questions about whether the war would end in 1944, rumors that intensified after the unsuccessful July 20 attempt to assassinate Hitler. George Marshall sent a message to commanders about possible redeployment of forces to the Pacific theater. Following his relief as commander in the west, when asked what the military should do, German Field Marshal Gerd von Rundstedt answered, "Make peace, you fools."[1]

Eisenhower gave in to the festive mood as well. "The German Army in the West has suffered a signal defeat in the campaign of the Seine and the

Loire at the hands of the combined Allied Forces," he wrote his commanders on August 29. "The enemy is being defeated in the East, in the South and in the North; he has experienced internal dissension and signs are not wanting that he is nearing collapse."[2]

Unlike many of his cohorts, though, Eisenhower hedged his bets. The enemy had not yet been defeated, and he knew the Germans had yet to fall back to their elaborate system of defenses along the Siegfried Line at the German borders, where they could regroup and prepare for the Allied assault on their homeland. By then the supply lines feeding the Allies would need replenishment.

He wrote Mamie on August 11, "Don't be misled by the papers. Every victory, even a partial one, is sweet—but the end of the war will come only with complete destruction of the Hun forces. So—always be optimistic and courageous, but not unduly expectant!"[3]

He argued to Mamie that the exaggerated claims for victory demeaned the sufferings of the men at the front who had to continue fighting and dying before the hostilities terminated. He confided to her that the question of when the war would end "usually makes me angry, because you can be certain this war is not 'won' for the man that is shivering, suffering and dying up on the Siegfried Line."[4]

If he had to contend with overoptimism only, Eisenhower might have slept better, but the rivalry among Allied commanders added to his problems. In those heady days of late summer, Montgomery and Patton vied for supplies and replacements and each contended he could, if his arm was adequately supported and the other's halted, smash through the defenses at the German border and end the war. They asked Eisenhower, in effect, to abandon the broad-front strategy devised before Overlord began and commit instead to a single powerful thrust into Germany.

It seemed that Eisenhower was daily besieged by one commander or the other—at times Bradley joined in on Patton's behalf—demanding to be given free rein to head to Berlin. Eisenhower could deal more bluntly with Patton because of their longstanding friendship and because, as the supreme commander and a fellow American, Eisenhower could more readily send Patton home if Patton refused to cooperate.

Eisenhower did not enjoy the same freedom with Montgomery, the commander who triumphed over the Germans at El Alamein when defeatism prevailed in Great Britain. With that victory, he single-handedly turned the war around for his nation and earned its everlasting acclaim. Eisenhower could disagree with Montgomery, but it would be near impossible to send him home in disgrace. Eisenhower's son, John, after visiting his father and witnessing different meetings with subordinates, wrote that "compared to Monty, Patton was no problem at all."[5] Eisenhower frequently spoke several times a day to Bradley, often communicated with Patton, but maintained minimal correspondence with the British commander.

Montgomery employed his vast brilliance to persuade Eisenhower that his strategy would gain the most at the least cost. The British favored a single powerful thrust against Germany rather than a broad front because of severe manpower shortages in the British Isles. They could not throw thousands of men into battle, so they preferred to use deception and intricate planning. On the other hand, the Americans could rely on brute force and enormous supply advantages to overwhelm their enemies. As historian Stephen Ambrose summed it up, Montgomery wanted to outthink the Germans while Eisenhower wanted to outfight them.[6]

Montgomery also contended that if the Allies favored Eisenhower's broad-front concept, they would never assemble sufficient forces anywhere along the line to crack through the vaunted German defenders. Better to organize a potent thrust at a single locale. The problem for the Americans was that, as had been the case in North Africa and Sicily, Montgomery moved very slowly.

Montgomery argued with a vehemence that irritated Eisenhower. He claimed that the British commander was "very conceited [and] so proud of his success to date that he will never willingly make a single move until he is absolutely certain of success—in other words, until he has concentrated enough resources that anybody could practically guarantee the outcome."[7]

For his part, Montgomery asserted that Eisenhower dismissed his ideas because of personal animosity. He claimed that he faced uphill battles because of "the feeling that existed against me among staff at Supreme Headquarters." He added that, "It was always very clear to me that Ike and I were poles apart when it came to the conduct of the war."[8]

To keep his armies moving, Eisenhower resorted to a bit of trickery. When meeting with Montgomery, he appeared to agree to his requests and diverted whatever spare supplies he could to keep Montgomery going in the north. If Patton then showed up at his doorstep, Eisenhower took the same approach. He rarely assented to everything they wanted, but he gave them just enough to keep them happy.

Montgomery and Patton had to worry about their own sectors only, while Eisenhower's responsibility was to the entire operation. Eisenhower believed the broad-front strategy helped achieve unity more than a single thrust favoring one commander over another.

One of Churchill's aides, Harold Macmillan, wrote of Eisenhower that, "he has two great qualities which make him much easier to deal with than many superficially better-endowed American or British generals. First, he will always listen to and try to grasp the point of an argument. Second, he is absolutely fair-minded and, if he has prejudices, never allows them to sway his final judgment. Compared with the wooden heads and desiccated hearts of many British soldiers I see here, he is a jewel of broad-mindedness and wisdom."[9]

To attain Allied unity, Eisenhower employed every tactic he could imagine with his tempestuous subordinates. More than once Montgomery thought the main effort was going to be in his region to the north, only to learn after he left the meeting with the supreme commander that Bradley and Patton were to maintain their offensive to the south.

Though Montgomery and Patton tested Eisenhower's patience throughout 1944 and 1945 and he often flirted with the notion of replacing them, Eisenhower was determined to keep the alliance intact. Besides, he hated the thought of waging war without Patton at his side, and he knew he could not simply remove Montgomery. The best alternative was to keep both men fighting, no matter what subterfuge he had to employ. Eisenhower had become a far more diplomatic leader now than during his days in North Africa.

Eisenhower had learned that a commander in modern warfare frequently faces as many concerns off the battlefield as on. He must develop the ability to make every commander, of any nation, feel a part of the team and that what they do is important.

Some have criticized Eisenhower for not being more explicit in expressing his wishes to Montgomery and Patton. In dealing with his soldiers in the 15th Infantry before the war, for instance, Eisenhower could issue direct commands, but that was a lieutenant colonel talking to his battalion, not a supreme commander dealing with generals who felt they were at least as talented as their superior. At such a high level of operation, Eisenhower had to rely on diplomacy over directness.

Patton and Bradley also criticized Eisenhower for being too easily swayed, claiming that whoever saw Eisenhower last was the commander who attained what he wanted. However, much the same was said of Roosevelt, who is recognized as a master politician. Churchill said of Eisenhower that "he supervised everything with a vigilant eye, and no one knew better than he how to stand close to a tremendous event without impairing the authority he had delegated to others."[10]

An incident during a September meeting with Montgomery illustrated how much abuse Eisenhower had to suffer to keep his broad front going. Montgomery questioned some of Eisenhower's decisions, calling them "rubbish." Eisenhower listened quietly for a time, then leaned over, put his hand on Montgomery's knee, and said, "Steady, Monty. You can't speak to me like that. I'm your boss."[11] Earlier in the war Eisenhower had thought nothing of sending home in disgrace any American officer who made derogatory comments about the British, yet he was willing to listen to such remarks against himself for the sake of unity.

Kay Summersby once asked Eisenhower why he put up with Montgomery's antics. He gave a simple reply that explained his command style in Europe. "If I can keep the team together, anything's worth it."[12]

In an August 23 meeting with Montgomery, Eisenhower agreed to divert additional supplies to the northern arm. When Bradley and Patton heard about it, they met with Eisenhower on September 2 and asked for complete support for a drive into Germany from Patton's direction in the south. Eisenhower refused to halt Montgomery's operations to please his fellow Americans, but he did order additional supplies, especially gasoline, to Patton's units.

Eisenhower could not have done much to alter the situation anyway. What slowed Montgomery and Patton was logistics, not Eisenhower. Allied planners had envisioned a gradual progression across France, with the Germans mounting a strong defense at each major river. These pauses in the advance of the front would permit Eisenhower to move up his supply lines from Normandy and seize new ports through which additional material could be brought in to support the next step.

But events did not unfold according to plan. The slow gains of June, when the Allied forces labored to break out of Normandy, created a huge backlog of supplies in England. Suddenly, Patton burst out to the south and reached the Seine, the first major river, eleven days earlier than expected. The situation changed overnight. Tons of supplies were waiting on British docks but the Allies were unable to rush necessary ammunition and gasoline to the front.

Eisenhower had to decide whether to halt at the Seine and bring the supply lines forward, or allow Patton and Montgomery to continue to advance until they ran out of supplies. He filtered enough supplies to both commanders to maintain pressure on the Germans all along the line for as long as possible.

Beetle Smith wrote after the war that "a hazard greater than the now thoroughly routed Germans was troubling us—supply."[13] Eisenhower had to slow the drive across France until additional ports were taken and sufficient supplies were made available. No matter how vehemently either man argued, Eisenhower could do little to meet both their needs. As he wrote Marshall on August 24, he wanted to push through into Germany as swiftly as Montgomery or Patton, but "there is no point in getting there until we are in a position to do something about it."[14] He added that each division operated with only one day's allotment of supplies rather than the usual five.

Two weeks later, Eisenhower further explained the predicament to Marshall. "The fact is that we are stretched to the absolute limit in maintenance both as to intake and as to distribution after supplies are landed." He added, "From the start we have always known that we would have to choose, after breaking out of the original bridgehead, some line which would mark a relative slackening in offensive operations while we improved maintenance facilities and prepared for an offensive operation that could be sustained for another indefinite period."

Eisenhower had a clear answer for the criticism from his commanders. Regarding Montgomery, he wrote to Marshall that the British commander "became obsessed with the idea that his Army Group could rush right on into Berlin provided we gave him all the maintenance that was in the theater—that is, immobilize all other divisions and give their transport and supplies to his Army Group, with some to Hodges [commander of the U.S. First Army]. Examination of this scheme exposes it as a fantastic idea."[15]

Had he been able to divert all the supplies needed to either Montgomery or Patton, a single thrust deep into Germany would not have succeeded. Now fighting on their own soil rather than in a foreign country, German defenders would battle with more determination and could attack the unit from the flanks as it progressed. Eisenhower later wrote in his memoirs, "Even had such a force been able to start with a total of ten or a dozen divisions—and it is certain no more could have been supported even temporarily—the attacking column would have gradually grown smaller as it dropped off units to protect its flanks and would have ended up facing inescapable defeat. Such an attempt would have played into the hands of the enemy."[16]

Subsequent events proved Eisenhower correct. It required another eight months before Germany succumbed to the combined efforts of the British and Americans to the west and the Russians to the east. As the fighting churned its way into Germany proper, hundreds of thousands of casualties mounted as the defenders fought and died at their posts.

Because of the severe supply shortages, Montgomery's chief of staff, Major General Sir Francis de Guingand, agreed with Eisenhower's action. De Guingand thought that a small-scale push might have registered gains, but nothing on the grand scale advocated by Montgomery or Patton would have succeeded.

—+≡—≡+—

Eisenhower veered from the broad-front policy only once, with drastic consequences. On September 10, Montgomery convinced Eisenhower that if he possessed the resources, he could drive across the Lower Rhine River at Arnhem in Holland. Eisenhower had three reasons for agreeing to this: he sought a bridgehead across the Rhine River before the Germans had time to reinforce their lines in the region; the assault might outflank the Siegfried Line of defenses that guarded the German border; and he hoped that this operation would prod the normally methodical and slow-moving Montgomery into a major offensive.

The operation, code-named Market-Garden, began on September 17. However, a speedy German reaction, and an overambitious Allied plan that required air assaults to coordinate with ground advances, led to a hasty setback.

Though he shifted additional supplies to Montgomery, Eisenhower declined to order Patton or other American commanders to halt their operations. Some struggled through swamps and forests to Montgomery's immediate south in support of Market-Garden, while Patton continued to push his armored divisions forward, although at a slower pace.

One negative consequence of Market-Garden was that in mounting the operation, Eisenhower delayed the Allied drive to seize the important port of Antwerp, a vibrant terminal that outproduced all other ports previously seized. Before D-Day, Allied planners emphasized Antwerp's importance in maintaining the push into Germany, and if any significant progress toward ending the war in 1944 was to be made, the port had to be controlled by mid-September. Market-Garden diverted so many Allied units that Antwerp was not secured until November 28, and by then horrible wintry weather destroyed any chances of rushing to Berlin by the end 1944.

Market-Garden should never have occurred. Eisenhower, perhaps weary from the barrage of requests coming from his British commander, succumbed to Montgomery's demand to switch the Allied focus to his northern arm. Though a temporary move, Eisenhower weakened Allied efforts elsewhere, particularly at Antwerp, and handed Patton and Bradley additional reason to doubt his management.

Much like a parent trying to mediate among quarreling children, Eisenhower spent an inordinate amount of time maintaining a shaky alliance threatened by the bombastic statements of Montgomery and Patton. As Eisenhower attempted to resolve this, Hitler unleashed one final surprise attack.

CHAPTER 13

"A Soldiers' War"

SINCE THE BEGINNING OF THE WESTERN EUROPEAN CAMPAIGN, Eisenhower had believed he would have the chance to engage the German Army west of the Rhine River. Hitler proved near Mortain that he would not yield ground once he held it, and that suggested he would likely send his forces out again to meet the Allied advance as it neared Germany. Eisenhower saw this as an opportunity. Another defeat would send the German forces reeling back in disarray to their border and would open Germany to the final Allied thrust.

Eisenhower now faced a serious predicament. He was poised to hit Germany's borders, but a precipitous drop in the number of troop replacements sent to him threatened to retard the Allied march into Germany. American factories worked overtime to produce the weaponry of war, yet where were the men to use the equipment?

"I don't know what the young manhood of America is doing," George Patton complained to Omar Bradley on December 3, 1944, "but they certainly are not appearing over here." He needed 9,000 men right away to adequately continue his assault toward Germany. Bradley blamed the optimistic outlooks as part of the problem. "I would suppose that somebody in Washington had made a wrong guess as to the date on which this war will be over,"[1] he told Patton.

Kay Summersby had seen her boss angry before, but she remarked that in early December Eisenhower was "especially perturbed"[2] over the slow pace of reinforcements reaching him. He had to put men into the line fast if he was to keep the enemy off balance.

"As the infantry replacement problem became acute we resorted to every kind of expedient to keep units up to strength,"[3] Eisenhower wrote in his memoirs. He besieged Washington with requests to hasten the arrival of additional troops; he switched men from service units in the back and placed them at the front; he sent his personnel chief to Washington to plead for extra men; he ordered his headquarters to employ members of the Women's Army Corps and to hire as many civilians as possible for clerical work so that more soldiers would be free to head to the front lines.

One of the difficulties for a military commander is that the nation's mothers and fathers, once they sense the end of a conflict is near, want their sons and daughters home as quickly as possible. Aware of that desire, politicians will sometimes remove a portion of the forces from a commander's arsenal in hopes of appeasing voters. Eisenhower would have preferred to possess an overwhelming superiority in numbers and steamroll his way to victory, but he had to adapt to the available resources and improvise. Much the same occurred in the Vietnam War, when commanders were hampered by huge troop withdrawals.

Eisenhower's problem with troop replacements arose partly because of his broad-front strategy. Since Eisenhower wanted constant action all along the advance rather than a single powerful thrust, he required more men than usual. With the Pacific theater continually drawing more units and resources into the struggle against the Japanese, and with the talk of imminent victory over Hitler, the pipeline of troops heading toward Europe dwindled.

"As the winter wore on, our need for troops became so great and our long lines were so thinly manned," Eisenhower wrote, "that when the new regiments arrived each army commander frequently found it necessary, instead of replacing tired troops with the fresh ones, to assign a special sector to the new troops . . ."[4]

As a result, certain portions of the Allied line were held by undermanned, weary, or untested divisions, including the Ardennes, a forested region along the Belgian-German-French borders where Bradley's depleted troops operated. Even though the Germans had twice before used this region as an invasion route into France—most recently in 1940, indicating that success could be achieved there—Eisenhower and Bradley believed they could lightly man this sector while placing stronger forces elsewhere. The dangerous road network that wound through the Ardennes combined with the wintry weather made it an unlikely location for a German counterattack. Eisenhower wrote in his diary, "it was not deemed highly probable that the enemy would, in winter, try to use that region in which to stage a counteroffensive on a large scale."[5] Allied intelligence observed German movement in the region, but they explained it as Hitler preparing to defend his borders, not as the initial signs of an attack. Montgomery agreed. On December 16, the British commander concluded, "The enemy is at present fighting a defensive campaign on all fronts; his situation is such that he cannot stage major offensive operations."[6] Both men were wrong.

＋⊨══⊨＋

Three months earlier, Hitler had conducted a conference with a group of top generals. The officers had grown accustomed to the German dictator meddling in their arena, but what he said that day stunned them. "I have just made a momentous decision," he announced to the hushed crowd. "I shall go over to the counterattack, that is to say, here, out of the Ardennes, with the objective—Antwerp."[7]

Hitler outlined his plan. The German drive would push through American lines in the Ardennes—precisely against Bradley's weakened front—cross the Meuse River, and split the Allied armies in two by racing toward Antwerp, one hundred miles away. Hitler hoped that such a bold plan would nudge the British and Americans toward negotiating peace with him and he would be free to deal with Stalin to the east.

The towns of St. Vith in the northern half of the Ardennes and Bastogne in the southern portion appeared to be the keys to his surprise attack, for the major east-west roads converged at these spots. The Germans would have to fight through St. Vith to reach the Meuse and secure Bastogne to prevent Patton from moving up to Bradley's aid from the south.

Hitler explained that an immense deception campaign would be implemented to fool the Allies into thinking an attack would occur elsewhere. Troop movements north of the Ardennes would draw attention to that sector, in addition to fake radio and telephone messages that would further entice the Allies to look to the north. Hitler issued strict orders about maintaining secrecy and threatened death to any officer who divulged details of his plan.

The German commanders were not convinced by Hitler's strategy. After the war, the commander of the 6th Panzer Army, General Josef Dietrich, whose forces played a prominent role in the Ardennes counterattack, explained the near-impossible tasks assigned him. His sarcasm illustrates the lack of belief in Hitler's plan for a counterattack: "All I had to do was to cross the river, capture Brussels and then go on and take the port of Antwerp. And all of this in December, January, and February, the worst three months of the year; through the Ardennes where snow was waist deep and there wasn't room to deploy four tanks abreast, let alone six armored divisions; when it didn't get light until eight in the morning and was dark again at four in the afternoon and my tanks can't fight at night; with divisions that had just been re-formed and were composed chiefly of raw untrained recruits; and at Christmas time."[8]

+>=—=<+

December 16 started off well for Eisenhower. He learned that he had been promoted to General of the Army, which placed him on an equal footing with Marshall and MacArthur, and he attended the wedding of a member of his staff. After the festivities, he left for a meeting with Bradley.

As the two discussed war matters, SHAEF's intelligence officer, Major General Kenneth Strong, walked into the room with information that the Germans had attacked in the Ardennes. Bradley dismissed it as a spoiling attack, but Eisenhower immediately recognized its significance.

"That's no spoiling attack,"[9] he said. He explained the Ardennes did not have enough American troops to make a diversionary attack worth the effort, and the Allies were too strong elsewhere for the Germans to launch a drive at any other location. This had to be the major German attack west of the Rhine that Eisenhower expected.

"I immediately ordered the cessation of all attacks and the gathering up of every possible reserve to strike the penetration in both flanks,"[10] he wrote in his diary. He reeled off a series of commands to contain and defeat the advance. Eisenhower first sent forces rushing toward the Ardennes from both the north and the south. He ordered two divisions that had been recuperating after Market-Garden, the 82nd and the 101st Airborne Divisions, to speed to the Ardennes as reinforcements, and told Bradley to detach the 10th Armored Division from Patton's drive toward Germany and rush it north toward the German attack. In the meantime, Bradley's thin line would have to slow the German army until help arrived. Eisenhower's major concern centered on the weather, as snow and overcast skies grounded his air arm. He could neither harass the Germans from the skies nor drop supplies to the Americans until the weather cleared.

Eisenhower displayed firm decisiveness at this meeting. Had he waited to gather additional intelligence before issuing his orders, he would have handed the Germans more time to puncture through Bradley's thin line. When Bradley told him that Patton would object to losing a division right in the middle of his own drive, Eisenhower snapped, "Tell him that Ike is running this goddamned war!"[11] This was the opportunity to inflict a costly defeat on the Germans, just as he had done near Falaise earlier in the war.

Eisenhower's mastery of the crisis was evident at a December 19 meeting of senior commanders near the city of Verdun. The outlook was not good: the Germans had attained early successes and forced the Americans to drop back toward St. Vith and Bastogne; uncooperative skies had neutralized his air power; and reinforcements moved slowly in the miserable wintry conditions. Eisenhower looked at his commanders, noticed the pessimistic mood, and opened the meeting with, "The present situation is to be regarded as one of opportunity for us and not of disaster. There will be only cheerful faces at this conference table."[12]

As usual, Patton replied with typical bravado, "Hell, let's have the guts to let the sons of bitches go all the way to Paris. Then we'll really cut 'em up and chew 'em up." Eisenhower smiled at his friend's enthusiasm, but admonished the crowd that the Germans must not reach the Meuse River.

Eisenhower then asked each commander to state the earliest that he could extract his forces from the line, turn them toward the Ardennes, and attack. Most hesitated, but Patton answered he could begin in two days with three divisions.

"Don't be fatuous, George,"[13] Eisenhower said angrily, for he thought what Patton suggested was clearly impossible. Patton explained that he had already had his staff draw up plans for such an emergency, and that he would be ready on December 21. After a brief discussion, Eisenhower told Patton to get the divisions rolling. Two of Patton's three army corps would halt their attacks in the south and head north to support Bradley's troops.

Eisenhower had stood by Patton after the slapping incident and rescued the general's career at a time when many wanted his scalp. Now Patton was coming to Eisenhower's rescue.

Eisenhower had to temporarily alter the command lines because the German advance had cut off Bradley's headquarters with his troops toward the north. Unable to adequately communicate with those units, Bradley could not conduct a proper defense. Eisenhower shifted the First and Ninth U.S. Armies to Montgomery's command and ordered Bradley to supervise Patton's movements in the south.

Bradley hated to lose control of the troops, especially to Montgomery, but admitted that it was the proper step to take. Eisenhower assured him that the First Army would return to his command as soon as possible, and that the Ninth Army would be restored when Montgomery's and Bradley's armies linked up beyond the Rhine River.

Eisenhower's Order of the Day for the soldiers battling the Germans in the frigid winter conditions indicated the supreme commander's faith in the man on the line. He did not have to explain the reasons for fighting or why they had to halt the enemy in the Ardennes—the men already understood the desperate conditions they faced. Instead, he focused on conveying confidence to a group of young infantrymen.

"So I call upon every man, of all the Allies, to rise now to new heights of courage, of resolution, and of effort," the order read. "Let everyone hold before him a single thought—to destroy the enemy on the ground, in the air, everywhere—destroy him."[14]

Like the soldiers Eisenhower had commanded earlier in his career, the weary Americans in the Ardennes rewarded Eisenhower's trust in their capabilities. The 101st Airborne arrived near Bastogne as the Germans approached and mounted a heroic defense. On December 23 and 24 the skies cleared over the besieged men, which permitted aircraft to parachute badly needed ammunition, food, and water to the troops. By December 26, when Patton's and other American units joined with the lines at Bastogne to lift the siege, Hitler's gamble had failed. Although fighting continued into January, when the First and Third Armies joined in Belgium and cut off the German retreat route, the battle had been settled by the end of December.

Eisenhower was so impressed with the performance of the American soldiers in the Ardennes that he wrote in his memoirs in 1967 that the gallant stand at Bastogne "was repeated in scores of little places, hamlets and bridge crossings and road bends, where handfuls of men might for hours hold up a Nazi column." He added that while he issued the orders and orchestrated the American response, "These were the times when the grand strategy and the high hopes of high command became a soldiers' war, sheer courage, and the instinct for survival."[15]

+>=<+

By year's end, Eisenhower's confidence in Montgomery all but disappeared. He had ignored the British commander's criticism for months in an effort to maintain harmony, but Montgomery's actions in late December 1944 and in January 1945 created an irreparable chasm between the two.

With the coming assault into Germany at hand, Montgomery lobbied to be named sole commander of a single thrust from the north. Weary of having his broad-front strategy challenged, Eisenhower lashed back, much as an exasperated parent does when a child has pushed too far.

Montgomery's chief of staff, Major General de Guingand, sensed Eisenhower's irritability when he walked into Eisenhower's headquarters for a meeting in late December. Eisenhower handed him a letter he intended to send to Marshall indicating that as Montgomery was displeased with his actions, he would ask the Combined Chiefs of Staff to decide whether to keep Montgomery or himself. It appeared obvious that the two could no longer work together.

"I was stunned by what I read," de Guingand explained in a television interview years after the war. "In very direct language it made it crystal-clear that a crisis of the first magnitude was indeed here."[16] De Guingand realized that if they were faced with the problem, the Combined Chiefs would have no choice but to support the American commander in an American-fueled campaign. He promised to talk to Montgomery and begged Eisenhower to refrain from sending the letter.

Eisenhower's tactic worked. De Guingand returned to Montgomery's headquarters and explained to his superior that Montgomery was going to be fired unless he stopped making unreasonable demands. Stunned by the turn of events—"I don't think I had ever seen him so deflated,"[17] wrote de Guingand—Montgomery asked, "Freddy, what should I do?"[18]

De Guingand suggested he swallow his pride and compose a contrite letter to Eisenhower. Beginning with an affable "Dear Ike," Montgomery wrote that he had meant no disrespect to the commander and "you can rely on me one hundred per cent to make it work . . ." He ended by writing that he was distressed that his views "may have upset you"[19] and asked Eisenhower to disregard his previous demands.

That storm had barely passed when Montgomery complicated matters again. On January 7 he boasted to the press that he, not Eisenhower, had taken action first in the Ardennes and that he had saved the day. Bradley and Patton exploded at what they considered an outrageous slur on the American soldier, and Bradley threatened to resign should he have to serve under Montgomery at any stage of the war. "This incident caused me more distress and worry that did any similar one of the war,"[20] Eisenhower later wrote in his memoirs, for the British commander had slighted not only

Eisenhower's role in the Ardennes but, more importantly, the role of the American infantrymen.

In this instance, Eisenhower checked his impulse to fire back at Montgomery. American commanders refused to cooperate with Montgomery, but Eisenhower still had to deal with the difficult Englishman. He waited for the furor to die down until a solution arose.

Fortunately, Winston Churchill came to Eisenhower's defense and ended the episode on January 18 by delivering in the House of Commons a ringing tribute to the Americans. He stated that the actions of the American soldiers in the Battle of the Bulge comprised "the greatest American battle of the war and will, I believe, be regarded as an ever famous American victory."[21]

The victory in the Ardennes, called the Battle of the Bulge for the shape the German salient in the American lines, involved 600,000 American soldiers, more than three times the number involved at Gettysburg in the Civil War. Against 77,000 American casualties, the Germans lost 82,000 soldiers who would later be sorely missed in battle once the Allies crossed the Rhine. The outcome of the Battle of the Bulge made the subsequent push through Germany's defenses along the Siegfried Line and the Rhine much easier, and it validated Eisenhower's belief that he could inflict another defeat on the Germans before the Allies reached the Rhine. The fighting in the West helped the Russian ally by drawing German forces away from the eastern front and, as superiors in Washington realized the war in Europe was not yet over, new replacements were sent to the front line.

Two factors contributed to victory in the Ardennes—the infantryman and Eisenhower. The American soldier had come far since the uneven performance in North Africa. Beetle Smith later wrote, "There in the snow and the mud, the American soldier proved himself invincible, and his resistance drained Germany dry of her precious reserves. Through all the remaining campaigns leading to the final surrender, the toll of the Ardennes was apparent in Germany's waning military power in the West."[22]

Eisenhower's career-long belief in the American soldier reaped dividends in the Ardennes. The soldiers knew their commander trusted them, and they responded with a superior performance. The same would be true of the Korean, Vietnam, and Iraqi conflict. A leader's faith in his forces produces exceptional effort from men and women under his command.

Smith was equally effusive in his praise for Eisenhower. He wrote that, "it was General Eisenhower's estimate of the situation and the swift decision to rush reinforcements to flanking key points which robbed the enemy of success." He added, "had the Supreme Commander waited to judge the scale of the attack before acting, our task would have been far more costly in lives when the moment came for our own counterattack."[23]

The Ardennes illustrated the success of Eisenhower's mature command style. He had remained supportive to Patton, and he believed that an officer's prime weapon—his soldiers—should be valued and recognized. When the chips were down in the Ardennes, both Patton and the American soldier came through.

Leave it to Eisenhower, however, to nudge the spotlight away from himself and onto the American infantryman. He recognized that the true sacrifices during the war were made not by him or any other commander but by the soldier. He wrote that the men had cast off cold, hunger, fear, and weariness to halt the Ardennes thrust. "They had given up their wives and children, or set aside their hope of wives and children, overcome luxuries or poverty, fought down their own inclinations to rest their tired bodies, to play it safe, to search out a hiding place."[24]

Few commanders throughout history have written so movingly of the men who fought for them. Eisenhower acknowledged his role in defeating the Germans, but he never forgot the men who struggled in the mud or snow, in the desert sands or mountain valleys.

CHAPTER 14

"The Mission Was Fulfilled"

BY THE END OF JANUARY 1945, EISENHOWER HAD CONCLUDED that German resistance could not last much longer. The fighting in the Ardennes had badly depleted Germany's troop pool, and with a mammoth Russian offensive hammering Hitler from the east, Eisenhower believed, as he later wrote in his memoirs, "that one more great campaign, aggressively conducted on a broad front, would give the death blow to Hitler Germany."[1] In order to maintain the momentum from the Ardennes, Eisenhower decided to launch his forces into action as quickly as possible. While Montgomery advanced in the north and part of Bradley's forces attacked in the center, other American units would surround and eliminate opposition in the Saar Basin to the south.

On February 8, 1945, Eisenhower began the campaign to clear the west side of the Rhine. A month of heavy fighting resulted in a succession of defeats for the enemy that stubbornly held on and fought, refusing to fall back across the Rhine and dig in along the eastern bank. From Montgomery in the north to Patton in the south, the Allies quickly advanced to the Rhine. When the final German defenses in the Saar were defeated later in March, all resistance west of the Rhine ceased. Since the heady days before June 6, 1944, when Hitler's iron grip extended from Berlin to the British Channel, the Germans had been forced back to their own borders. They now had to defend their homeland against ravaging attacks from both the east and the west.

"General Eisenhower's belief that the Germans would choose the fatal course of fighting till it was too late to withdraw, proved correct in every instance except one," Beetle Smith wrote after the war. "At Cologne the enemy retreated across the river with forces intact."[2] At Falaise and again in the Ardennes, Eisenhower had seen the enemy fight until all hope was gone, even when, as he told a press conference, "any sensible soldier would have gone back to the Rhine." He explained that once ensconced in sturdy defenses along the river, they could have "stood there and said, 'Now try to come across.'"[3] Instead, the Germans suffered for their stubbornness, losing 250,000 men as prisoners plus thousands more wounded or dead.

Eisenhower thought that Allied success west of the Rhine justified his sticking to his broad-front strategy in spite of the demands of Montgomery, Patton, and others. As he wrote George Marshall on March 26, "The point is that the great defeats, in some cases almost complete destruction, inflicted on the German forces west of the Rhine, have left him [Hitler] with very badly depleted strength to man that formidable obstacle [the Rhine]. It was those victories that made possible the bold and relatively easy advances that both First and Third Armies are now making toward Kassel. I hope this does not sound boastful, but I must admit to a great satisfaction that the things that Bradley and I have believed in from the beginning and have carried out in the face of some opposition both from within and without, have matured so splendidly."[4]

He now planned to halt his armies along the Rhine, bring up the supply lines and reinforcements, and prepare for the last thrust into Germany. A solitary bridge at Remagen, however, altered his plans.

With his armies in the west retreating toward Germany's borders, Hitler counted on an extended defense along the Rhine River to slow the enemy and give him time to prepare for the final battle on home soil. He ordered the destruction of every bridge crossing the Rhine and threatened that should the Allies capture a bridge intact, the commander of that area would be shot.

Eisenhower expected to pause at the river as well, but a March 7 telephone call from Bradley alerted him to an opportune moment. Bradley had been talking to the visiting Major General Harold Bull of SHAEF (Supreme Headquarters Allied Expeditionary Force) when General Courtney Hodges of the First Army informed him that a bridge still stood at the town of Remagen, Germany, south of the Ruhr. "Shove everything you can across it, Courtney," Bradley told his commander, "and button the bridgehead up tightly."

General Bull advised Bradley against the move. He claimed that the Americans would run directly into stiff German opposition, and argued that the overall plan for advance called for a methodical crossing of the river all along the line as opposed to a single weak thrust across. Irritated at Bull's timidity, Bradley called Eisenhower to seek confirmation for his actions. "Hold on to it, Brad," Eisenhower almost shouted into the phone. "Get across with whatever you need—but make certain you hold that bridgehead."[5] Thus bolstered by Eisenhower's support, Bradley sent the Americans across and a valuable toehold on the east side of the wide Rhine River was soon expanded to a bridgehead twenty miles long and eight miles deep. Hitler would no longer be able to mount a protracted defense on Germany's western border.

"Our troops are solidly across the Rhine—something that is a great satisfaction to me," an ecstatic Eisenhower later wrote Mamie. The moment caused him to think of the future. "Boy, will I be glad when this is all over . . . Wish I knew how long it will be."[6]

Now ensconced on the east side of the Rhine, Eisenhower turned to the final steps in the destruction of the German military. Following the broad-front strategy that had characterized his march across France,

Eisenhower called for an assault to the north of the resource-rich Ruhr region by Montgomery and an American attack to the Ruhr's south by Hodges and Patton. After the two armies closed behind the Ruhr and cut it off from the rest of Germany, his armies would methodically plunge deeper into the country until the enemy surrendered. The task sounded simpler than it was, for the enemy was certain to fight with more determination now in his own land.

The drive commenced on March 24 when Allied divisions rushed along the Ruhr's northern and southern flanks. Eisenhower issued a proclamation to the local populations describing the situation for the German nation as hopeless. He called for the surrender of German soldiers and suggested that the German people begin planting crops. Not surprisingly, the plea fell on deaf ears. "My purpose was to bring the whole bloody business to an end," Eisenhower later wrote. "But the hold of Hitler on his associates was still so strong and was so effectively applied elsewhere, through the medium of the Gestapo and SS, that the nation continued to fight."[7]

Though he wished for the war to be over quickly, especially now that the outcome was no longer uncertain, Eisenhower still had to wipe out the last traces of German military might before the nation ceased fighting. "We've got another battle in progress—prospects look good," he wrote Mamie in March, "but I never count my Germans until they're in our cages, or are buried!"[8]

In mid-April the First and Ninth American Armies met in Lippstadt, Germany. This action completed the encirclement of the Ruhr and trapped more than 300,000 German soldiers who were forced to surrender.

At the same time, Montgomery had headed into Holland and Denmark, while to the south American units had seized Nuremberg and Munich. Hitler's empire was crumbling faster than expected.

Despite favorable progress, Eisenhower's woes continued as his top commanders persisted with their outrageous behavior. Eisenhower watched in amusement and irritation as Montgomery and Patton urged their respective troops forward so they could have the honor of being the first to cross the Rhine. Montgomery had even halted a drive by an American division under his command so he could lead troops across first. "Sometimes when I get tired of trying to arrange the blankets smoothly over several prima donnas in the same bed," he confided to Marshall in March, "I think no one person in the world can have so many illogical problems."[9] He could have put an end to the tempestuous actions with blunt directives, but Eisenhower continued to leave considerable autonomy to his able, but emotional, commanders.

The bickering, added to the normal pressures that came with his job, took their toll on Eisenhower. His bright smile appeared less frequently, and his staff felt the sting of occasional tirades. Smith became so concerned for Eisenhower's health that he insisted Ike take a brief vacation. "Look at you," he told his commander. "You've got bags under your eyes. Your blood pressure's higher than it's ever been, and you can hardly walk across the room."[10] Eisenhower agreed to a five-day break in Cannes in March, which briefly reinvigorated his spirits.

Eisenhower felt more comfortable when his headquarters moved from the ornate trappings of Versailles to a simple building in Reims, closer to the front. He never enjoyed working amidst luxury, and now he could more readily include one of his favorite pastimes in his schedule. "General Eisenhower was constantly appearing in the front lines . . . ,"[11] Smith wrote after the war.

Instead of listening to a litany of complaints, as Eisenhower often did with his commanders, he heard optimism from the soldiers. "The men remember the situation existing when we started shipping this Army to France three years ago," he wrote Marshall on April 27, "and recall the respect, if not awe, in which we then held the German fighting prowess. They regard their accomplishments with pride."[12]

During one visit along the Rhine, Eisenhower spotted a soldier. "How are you feeling, son?" he asked the private about an assault across the river.

"General, I'm awful nervous," the private replied.

"Well," Eisenhower said, "you and I are a good pair then, because I'm nervous too. But we've planned this attack for a long time and we've got all the planes, the guns, and airborne troops we can use to smash the Germans. Maybe if we just walk along together to the river we'll be good for each other."[13] With that, private and general strolled along the Rhine, drawing strength and comfort from each other's presence.

On April 12 Eisenhower inspected the Ohrdruf-Nord concentration camp, then followed with an April 13 examination of the infamous Buchenwald camp. Eisenhower had seen death and destruction, but nothing compared to the mounds of bodies he witnessed and the appalling stench he experienced. Patton, the hardened commander who lived for war, turned away in disgust and vomited at the sight of Hitler's victims. Eisenhower's part-time driver, Mickey McKeogh, wrote that he had never seen the supreme commander so mad. An enraged Eisenhower ordered that every soldier not on the front line was to walk through these camps so they had an idea of what they were fighting against. He wrote Marshall on April 15: "But the most interesting—although horrible—sight that I encountered during the trip was a visit to a German internment camp near Gotha. The things I saw beggar description." He added that, "The visual evidence and the verbal testimony of starvation, cruelty and bestiality were so overpowering as to leave me a bit sick. In one room, where they were [*sic*] piled up twenty or thirty naked men, killed by starvation, George Patton would not even enter."

He then explained why he had made a personal trip to the camps. "I made the visit deliberately, in order to be in position to give *first-hand* evidence of these things if ever, in the future, there develops a tendency to charge these allegations merely to 'propaganda.'"[14] Eisenhower was more prescient than he realized, as a small group of revisionist historians would later declare the Holocaust a myth. His firsthand observations combined with those of thousands of American soldiers who liberated the camps and the camp survivors stand as irrefutable evidence of Hitler's sordid attempt to annihilate the Jews and other groups.

He wrote of the incidents to Mamie, but his letter of the same day, while conveying similar anger, omitted the gruesome details. "The other day I visited a German internment camp. I never dreamed that such cruelty, bestiality, and savagery could really exist in this world! It was horrible."[15]

Another issue Eisenhower faced was what to do with Patton now that he had reached the Czechoslovakian border. The British Chiefs of Staff urged Eisenhower to immediately send Patton's forces into that country to grab Prague before the Russians accomplished the same feat, but Eisenhower ignored the advice. He was a soldier, not a politician, and he would not order his forces toward an objective unless it had military value. "I shall *not* attempt any move I deem militarily unwise merely to gain a political prize unless I receive specific orders from the Combined Chiefs of Staff,"[16] he wrote Marshall, who agreed with his commander.

The incident foreshadowed a more divisive dispute that would hound Eisenhower in the war's waning months and eventually turn into a source of contention for the rest of his life. Churchill had been lobbying Roosevelt and Marshall to keep the Allied armies going until they reached Berlin. Under the terms set at a meeting held at Yalta on the Black Sea, Roosevelt, Stalin, and Churchill agreed to partition Germany. The German capital fell under the Soviet zone of occupation. Now, with military events in the west unfolding so smoothly, Churchill argued against halting the American and British armies short of Berlin. He believed that in a postwar world, it would be better to keep Berlin in the hands of the West rather than in the hands of the Soviets.

Eisenhower flatly rejected such notions. He was a military leader with a military mission, and he would not be swayed by political reasons. He wrote Marshall on April 15 that rather than attack toward Berlin, he intended to place his forces in the middle of the country on the defensive while Montgomery advanced toward Denmark in the north and Patton swerved toward the Austrian Alps in the south. Rumors circulated that Hitler might retreat to the mountains of southern Bavaria and Austria with a sizable group of Nazi die-hards, where he would begin a protracted guerrilla-style warfare against the Allies. Eisenhower was eager to send forces south to destroy this national redoubt.

"I deem both of these [Denmark and Bavaria] to be vastly more important than the capture of Berlin—anyway, to plan for making an immediate effort against Berlin would be foolish in view of the relative situation of the Russians and ourselves at the moment. We'd get all coiled up for something that in all probability would never come off."[17] Even if he seized the capital, the Yalta agreement stipulated that he would have to hand it over to the Russians.

Eisenhower listed other reasons why he wanted to avoid Berlin. General Bradley estimated that the operation would cost a minimum of 100,000 casualties. Eisenhower also contended that Allied forces would have to care for thousands of prisoners of war, civilians, and displaced persons, with the Soviet army within 35 miles of Berlin while his rested 200 miles distant. Faced with brutal fighting in the Pacific, the last thing Eisenhower and Marshall wanted was a bitter campaign to seize the German capital. They planned to end the war in Europe as quickly as possible and begin transferring America's military might to the Pacific. As the Russians later lost 361,000 casualties in their drive against Berlin—a city defended by soldiers willing to obey Hitler's fight to the death order—Eisenhower's fears on this point proved valid.

John Eisenhower pointed out what he called an often-overlooked reason for his father's refusal to take Berlin. He contended that Roosevelt hoped to obtain Russian aid in fighting the Japanese, and this would have been impossible if the Americans had seized Berlin first. In the spring of 1945, a costly invasion of the four main Japanese islands still appeared necessary. Roosevelt wanted to bring a potent alliance with the Russians into the fight to end the Pacific war as speedily as possible.

But above all else, Eisenhower refused to take Berlin for one reason—it had no strategic value. "He was, and always considered himself, strictly a military commander . . . ,"[18] wrote Beetle Smith after the war. He had been given the goal of destroying the German war machine, and Berlin offered no such benefits.

"Every plan, decision, and purpose of the Allied command was determined always by one inflexible rule—'Destroy the German forces, speedily and completely,'" Smith wrote. He claimed that Berlin had no military value and Eisenhower's efforts elsewhere in Germany "had put an end to all German resistance in thirty-three climactic days by the only means [brute force] the Nazis would accept." Smith added that the only German military near Berlin were the forces designated to defend the capital, and "The Red Army could be counted on to take care of that job." He explained that, "Battles are fought to defeat armies, to destroy the enemy's ability to go on fighting."[19]

An attack toward Berlin would divert forces from their main objective, the destruction of the German military. Eisenhower argued that if you annihilate an enemy's armies, everything else will fall into place. Without an army in the field, Hitler could not draw out peace negotiations.

"Dad felt seriously that he'd been given a military objective: to defeat the armed forces of Germany," John Eisenhower said. "All of our military doctrine from the days at West Point emphasizes that the object of military operations is the enemy's armed forces, *not* cities."[20]

Another reason for avoiding Berlin was more typical of the unassuming commander. During his 1952 presidential campaign, Eisenhower responded to criticism that he had allowed Berlin to fall into communist hands by saying, with a trace of irritation, that none of his critics had to "go out and choose the ten thousand mothers whose sons would have been killed capturing a 'worthless objective.'"[21]

On April 11 the Ninth Army reached the Elbe River near Magdeburg, the agreed-upon spot where the Allied forces from the west would cease their offensives in Germany and meet their Russian cohorts. The war was almost over, but as long as Hitler breathed, opposition continued.

<hr>

April also brought the deaths of two of the major figures in the European war. On April 12, Roosevelt succumbed at his retreat in Georgia. His successor, Harry Truman, a man about whom Eisenhower knew little, would now orchestrate the war's end. Eighteen days later, with the Russian army closing in on his underground bunker in Berlin, Hitler committed suicide.

Despite the evidence that German resistance was weakening, Eisenhower and other Allied leaders continued to insist that the war would not end until Germany surrendered unconditionally, a stance that unified the Allied camp but gave little incentive for German military leaders to order their troops to lay down their arms. In addition to the fighting in Germany, combat still raged in Holland, Italy, and Denmark until shortly before the surrender.

On May 7, 1945, with all hope of resistance gone and with Hitler dead, the German military surrendered unconditionally. At 2:41 A.M.

General Alfred Jodl, representing the hastily formed German government that succeeded Hitler, arrived at Eisenhower's headquarters in Reims to surrender the nation to the Allies. While officials explained the terms of surrender to Jodl in one room, Eisenhower paced in his office. He did not want to see the German officer until he had agreed to every item.

Beetle Smith and others then escorted Jodl into Eisenhower's room. Eisenhower asked Jodl if he understood the terms, and warned Jodl that he would be held personally responsible for any violations. The German general agreed, bowed, and left.

A relieved Eisenhower then permitted photographers into his office, He grabbed the two pens Jodl used to sign the surrender document and crossed them into the "V" sign popularized earlier in the war by Winston Churchill. He and his staff toasted the occasion with champagne, and spent a few hours enjoying the moment they had worked so long to bring about.

Eisenhower had to draft the message announcing the end of hostilities. Commanders in other wars, cognizant that their words would be recorded for history, composed stirring declarations flowing with adjectives and adverbs, but Eisenhower remained true to his style. "The mission of this Allied force was fulfilled at 0241 local time, May 7, 1945."[22]

With those simple words, the man from Abilene terminated fighting in Europe. He had held the alliance together despite recriminations and in the face of immense opposition from monumental egos. He had not taken gun in hand and marched to the front line—although he most likely would have preferred to do so—but his steady leadership enabled millions of other men from diverse nations to do so and win.

Beetle Smith stated that of all the valuable contributions made to the war by his commander, Eisenhower's commitment to the alliance and to the broad-front strategy were his greatest. In eleven months of combat against Hitler, few changes were made to the general strategic plan. Eisenhower's belief in the plan, against bitter criticism, kept the Allied advance on track.

"Never once since our Headquarters came into being in London on February 12, 1944, had our unity of purpose been broken," wrote Smith in 1956. "We were a team of American and British officers, with nationality forgotten to an extent which could never be realized by any man who was not part of our daily striving." A coalition that transcends divisions and works toward a common goal achieves success more smoothly than one that does not, whether the partnership exists in modern warfare or in business.

Smith added, "The Anglo-American Staff functioned as a complete, integral unit under the Supreme Commander. At times we disagreed—naturally. But we disagreed frankly as individuals, not as Britons and Americans." In Smith's opinion, Eisenhower "was responsible for every decision . . ."[23] and as such, the commander who most contributed to victory.

At the war's end, Eisenhower looked forward to returning to his wife, settling down on a farm, and enjoying relaxing moments reading, fishing, and playing with his grandchildren. After all, once you have dismantled the most heinous dictatorship in history, what greater challenges could possibly lie ahead?

PART V

After the War

CHAPTER 15

"I Like Ike"

BEFORE HE TACKLED THE ISSUES FACING HIM AS COMMANDER OF occupied Germany, Eisenhower traveled to England and the United States. In both countries, crowds staged monumental demonstrations of their affection for the triumphant general.

On June 12, 1945, Eisenhower spoke at London's 600-year-old Guildhall, where he was named honorary citizen of the city. People shouted, "Ike, good old Ike!"[1] as he walked the streets and signed autographs, and inside the hall Churchill toasted the commander and said his contributions were and will continue to be "one of bringing our countries together in the much more difficult task of peace in the same way he has brought them together in the awful cataclysm of war."[2] Following the ceremony, Eisenhower headed to Buckingham Palace to receive the Order of Merit from King George VI.

Later that month, Eisenhower returned to the United States where he received even more acclaim. Throngs greeted him at Washington's airport with shouts of, "Ike, Ike."[3] A brief reunion with Mamie ended with Eisenhower being whisked to the Capitol to address a joint session of Congress. On June 19 four million New Yorkers packed Manhattan's streets to welcome the hero home, who then traveled to Abilene for a family reunion and a raucous hometown welcome. After years with world figures and noted officers, a humble Eisenhower told his fellow Kansans, "The proudest thing I can say today is that I am from Abilene."[4]

After an all-too-brief sojourn in the United States, Eisenhower returned to Germany to supervise the Allied occupation of the defeated nation. For six months he faced a series of issues, mainly how to transport soldiers home and what to do about former Nazis. Eisenhower ordered that each morning a list be placed on his desk detailing the numerous requests from soldiers to be sent home. He tried to accommodate as many as possible, but he had to balance the soldiers' wishes with the needs of the American military, which now considered communist Russia a likely antagonist and did not want to dismantle the immense wartime machine too hastily.

During one visit to a former German camp that housed American prisoners of war, Eisenhower listened to numerous complaints that the Americans were being sent home too slowly. Now that the war was over, couldn't he arrange for additional American troop transports? Eisenhower lacked the ships, but before he left he produced a solution—he could double the numbers aboard each transport by having the men eat and sleep in shifts. He talked to the men and said they could either continue the more leisurely pace and travel in relative comfort, or hasten the process by doubling up on the ships. When he asked, "Do you want to go back home conveniently—or would you rather double up, be uncomfortable, and get home quickly?"[5] the men's shouted response unanimously indicated the latter. Eisenhower ordered the steps be implemented.

A more troubling problem awaited Eisenhower—what to do with the millions of displaced persons now being held in Allied hands, especially Jews who had been confined in concentration camps. The conditions in Allied quarters, although considerably better than the German camps, still lacked the comforts of home. In some locations, Jews and other displaced persons huddled in rude barracks and ate simple fare while German civilians enjoyed warm quarters in their own homes.

Eisenhower was responsible for the care of 5.5 million people rather than the three million planned for, a situation that grossly stretched the capabilities in war-ravaged Europe. A study found that 56,000 of those millions perished, a one percent death rate that, under the harsh circumstances, was not as bad as it could have been.

A problem arose when General George Patton ignored an order to remove all former Nazi officials from office, contending that he needed their cooperation to maintain order. Perturbed that Patton would so blatantly ignore his dictates, Eisenhower bluntly admonished the warrior, "I demand you get off your bloody ass and carry out the denazification program as you are told instead of mollycoddling the goddamn Nazis!"[6]

But Patton further forced Eisenhower's hand when, in a speech, he stated that Nazis were little more than Republicans or Democrats. Eisenhower called Patton to his headquarters, where he shouted so loudly at the officer that staff members in another room could clearly hear his words. At long last, Eisenhower relieved his friend Patton from command of the Third Army and placed him in charge of compiling a study of the American war campaigns in Europe, removing Patton from the limelight.

<hr />

Eisenhower held three other jobs from 1945 to 1952. In the fall of 1945 George Marshall stepped down as Army chief of staff. Despite Eisenhower's objections to dealing with the politics of Washington, D. C., he assented to President Harry Truman's wishes like a good soldier and became the next chief of staff on November 19.

The man who had supervised the largest conglomeration of military might in the nation's history now had to implement its dismantling. Within eighteen months, the Army shrank from 12 million men to 1.5 million.

"I had a notion that I might settle down in the vicinity of some small college, and to make a connection that would bring me in touch with young people,"[7] Eisenhower wrote of his longstanding wishes to be a part of the educational world after retiring from the military. When New York's Columbia University inquired whether he would like to become its new president, Eisenhower at first wondered if they had not meant to contact his brother Milton, a renowned educator, instead of him. The university explained that he indeed was their choice and that Eisenhower's vast experiences and contacts would benefit Columbia. While the university was far from being a small college, Eisenhower relished the challenges of helming a large institution. In May 1948 he was named president of Columbia University.

Eisenhower's first step was to move the location of his office so that it was more accessible to students. His predecessor had worked in a library office that could only be reached by a private elevator, but Eisenhower moved it to the first floor, in plain sight. "Students, the chief reason for a university's being, and for me the paramount appeal and attraction in campus life, were in danger of becoming numerical figures on forms and passing, unknown faces on campus,"[8] he wrote in his memoirs.

University life was not the sole occupation during these years. Eisenhower wrote the best-selling *Crusade in Europe,* a memoir of his service in World War II, and on January 7, 1951, he took leave from Columbia to serve as the head of the North Atlantic Treaty Organization (NATO) for seventeen months.

✦━━✦

Two major questions concerned Eisenhower in 1951 and 1952—was he a Republican or a Democrat, and would he agree to run for president? Recognizing that the general's immense popularity would translate into millions of votes, both parties eagerly courted Eisenhower. He coyly declined to answer at first, still claiming that politics was nothing more than "a combination of gossip, innuendo, sly character assassination and outright lies"[9] that candidates used for their own benefit. Whether he honestly preferred to remain out of presidential race or cleverly remained aloof to increase his attractiveness is not clear.

In January 1952, Eisenhower announced that he was a Republican. Two months later, even though he had yet to declare that he was a candidate, he permitted his name to be placed on the New Hampshire primary ballot. When he easily defeated front-runner Senator Robert A. Taft of Ohio, Eisenhower left NATO to run for the nomination.

Eisenhower answered a series of questions from a skeptical press corp. When asked why had he decided to run when he detested politics, he replied that if the country needed him, he would again answer the call of duty. To one reporter who wondered what political training he had to make him a credible candidate, Eisenhower stated, "What the hell are you talking about? I have been in politics, the most active sort of politics, most of my adult life. There's no more active political organization in the world than the armed services of the U.S."[10] As far as experience in world affairs, he claimed he had seen more of the world and dealt with more prominent leaders than just about anybody.

Eisenhower ran a successful campaign to receive the Republican nod, bolstered by the slogan "I Like Ike," whose simplicity and directness summarized the candidate. After winning the nomination, Eisenhower broke tradition to visit his chief rival, Senator Taft. "I hope we can work together,"[11] he told Taft, continuing in politics the theme that prevailed during his military career.

One issue dominated the presidential campaign—the war in Korea. On June 25, 1950 communist-controlled North Korea invaded the democratic South Korea. The United States intervened and carried most of the war's burden, both in terms of soldiers committed and funds allocated, while the United Nations supplied the rest. Of the 520,000 troops sent to assist the South Korean forces from the war's outset, 90 percent were from the United States. People at home wondered why the country should risk so many soldiers and spend such vast sums of money when the rest of the world would only contribute 50,000 soldiers.

Eisenhower quickly took advantage of the public's disillusionment with Korea. On October 24, 1952, he stated in a nationally televised speech in Detroit, Michigan that if elected, he would travel to Korea to end the war. "The [presidency] requires a personal trip to Korea. I shall make that trip. Only in that way could I learn best how to serve the American people in the cause of peace. I shall go to Korea."[12]

Eisenhower never made it clear whether he intended to end the war militarily or diplomatically, but the prospect of the revered warrior resolving the situation appealed to the country. On election day 1952, voters over-whelmingly elected Eisenhower to be the next president.

Eisenhower kept his promise. On November 29, 1952, before as-suming the office of presidency, Eisenhower secretly traveled to Korea. While an arranged roster of dignitaries purposely visited Eisenhower's empty New York apartment to make it appear he was still there, the pres-ident-elect spent three days visiting the troops at the fighting front to learn firsthand what the situation was. After listening to the men in the field and their commanding officers, Eisenhower concluded that the United States faced only two options to end the war—either widen it through use of the atom bomb, which he dismissed, or attempt to negoti-ate a settlement that would return both North and South Korea to their prewar borders. He refused to permit the war with its inevitable casualties to drag on, so he decided that once in office, he would place his efforts toward a negotiated peace.

After being sworn in as president, Eisenhower moved quickly. He en-couraged the South Korean government to expand its armed forces to more than half a million so that the burden of conducting the war could gradu-ally be eased from the United States. He also instructed his negotiators in Korea to reach an agreement with the enemy as soon as possible.

Within a few months, Eisenhower had his wish. On July 27, 1953, more than three years after the beginning of the war, negotiators reached a settlement that returned the two Koreas to their prewar borders.

Those who celebrated the cease of hostilities did so more out of relief than exultation in the outcome. The United States could claim no clear-cut victory; the North Koreans had only been confined to their prewar borders, where they still, as communists, remained a threat to the democratic world. Americans took solace only in knowing that the killing had stopped.

"I was happy it was over," declared General Arthur Trudeau, the com-mander of the U.S. Army's 7th Division. "It was apparent that all we were going to do was sit there and hold positions. There wasn't going to be any victory. All we could do was go on losing more lives."[13]

As it was, the casualties were alarming. The United States had 33,629 dead and another 105,785 were wounded. A poll taken right after the end of the fighting showed that 62 percent of the American public believed the war had not been worth fighting. Eisenhower later listed his efforts to end the strife as one of his proudest accomplishments.

+⇒·⇒+

The Korean conflict marked merely the first in a series of foreign and domestic clashes that centered on communism. Even before Eisenhower gained the presidency, Wisconsin Senator Joseph R. McCarthy began his investigation into suspected communists inside the federal government. Among the senator's targets was George Marshall, whom he condemned for, among other supposed offenses, being under communist influence while serving as secretary of state and defense in the late 1940s and early 1950s.

Eisenhower declined to publicly censure McCarthy, even though he privately railed against the politician's tactics. He believed any censure of McCarthy should originate in the Senate, and he wrote to a friend in April 1954 that "nothing will be so effective in combating this particular kind of trouble-making as to ignore him. This he cannot stand."[14] Eisenhower was able to disregard Patton's and Montgomery's outbursts because he could easily assert his authority over them, but he did not have the same power over a senator. Disregarding the politician, which Eisenhower continued to do after becoming president, handed McCarthy an unchallenged arena in which to continue his investigations. The senator ruined the reputations of many people by simply claiming they were suspected communists.

A firmer stance by Eisenhower might have deflected some of McCarthy's accusations. His hands-off approach had worked during the war because while he dealt with strong-willed individuals pursuing their own agendas, the common goal of defeating Hitler united them. As president, Eisenhower lacked a similar bond with strong-willed politicians. He could not appeal to a higher cause with Senator McCarthy, and thus Eisenhower's silence acted against the country's interests.

Eisenhower stated as much when he wrote to George Marshall in 1952. "The whole atmosphere is so different from that to which soldiers of long service become accustomed that I sometimes find it difficult indeed to adjust myself."[15]

According to his son, John, Eisenhower later regretted that he did not rush more vigorously to the defense of Marshall. He did not realize that some would see this as a betrayal of a former military colleague who had been so influential for Eisenhower's Army career and had done so much for the nation.

In his foreign policy toward the Soviet Union, Eisenhower crafted a version of Theodore Roosevelt's "speak softly and carry a big stick" policy. He moved away from President Harry Truman's reliance on containing communism by stationing land forces at the periphery of Soviet power, and instead aimed to deter the spread of communism by publicizing that no weapon in the United States arsenal, including nuclear weapons, was ruled out.

At the same time Eisenhower advocated the pursuit of peace and collaboration. In what some believe is his finest speech as president, on April 16, 1953, Eisenhower described the costs of a nuclear arms race: "Every gun that is made, every warship launched, every rocket fired signifies, in the final sense, a theft from those who hunger and are not fed, those who are cold and are not clothed."[16] He added that the cost of one heavy bomber equaled the expense of building a new school in thirty cities, and a new destroyer consumed the same amount of money as housing for eight thousand people. "Under the cloud of threatening war," he stated, "it is humanity hanging from a cross of iron."[17] His plea for cooperation and a reduction in the spiraling arms race fell on deaf ears in the Soviet Union, but it gained Eisenhower acclaim around the world.

Though Eisenhower hoped to check the arms race, he made the first steps that committed American support to a war against communism in one part of the world and an undercover Central Intelligence Agency (CIA) role in another. In 1954, with the French losing control of its former colony of Vietnam to communist-supported forces, Eisenhower propounded the domino theory—the fall of the democratic South Vietnam to communism would result in nearby nations toppling into communist hands, one by one in a process that could only be stopped with American support of South Vietnam. While events later proved the domino theory wrong, Eisenhower's initial commitment in the Far East soared under subsequent presidents until a full-fledged war raged in the Southeast Asian country.

The other stage of engagement stood only ninety miles from the U.S. border. In 1959 Fidel Castro came to power in Cuba and aligned his country with the Soviet Union. With a communist regime so close to Florida, Eisenhower approved a CIA plan to support Cuban exiles in overthrowing Castro. The subsequent operation, called the Bay of Pigs, occurred under President John F. Kennedy, but the roots had been planted during Eisenhower's tenure.

A heightened sense of urgency occurred on October 3, 1957 when the Soviet Union successfully launched Sputnik, the world's first space satellite. Many in the United States panicked that the communists had beaten the United States into space, and noted scientist Edward Teller claimed the event was a greater tragedy than Pearl Harbor. In a series of televised speeches Eisenhower counseled patience. His calm demeanor and vigorous support of America's prowess belayed fears that swept across the nation.

Tension with the Soviet Union mounted in May 1960 when the Soviets shot down an American spy plane, the U–2, deep inside their territory. Eisenhower at first believed that the plane had accidentally crashed and denied Soviet accusations of spying on their nation. He claimed the craft was a weather plane that had simply drifted off course over Turkey and accidentally intruded on Soviet air space. When the Soviet Union produced the pilot and pieces of the spy plane on May 7, Eisenhower could do nothing but let the affair drop. In what he called "the stupid U–2 mess,"[18] Eisenhower lost prestige in certain parts of the world and saw his hopes for a summit with the Soviet leader, Nikita Khrushchev, disintegrate.

Eisenhower took a less visible stance in crucial domestic matters. In the *Brown v. Board of Education of Topeka* ruling on May 17, 1954, the Supreme Court declared unconstitutional the practice that existed in some southern states of having "separate but equal" school systems for blacks and whites. Henceforth, public schools were to be open to all students regardless of race.

Eisenhower believed that the Supreme Court had gone too far in the issue and should only have required equal opportunity rather than full-fledged integration, but once the court had spoken, he intended to enforce the law. He told a news conference, "The Supreme Court has spoken, and I am sworn to . . . the constitutional process . . . I will obey."[19]

His first test came in 1957 when Arkansas governor Orval Faubus employed the National Guard to prevent nine black students from enrolling at Little Rock's Central High School. When a white mob surrounded the school a few days later, the city's mayor asked Eisenhower to send aid. The president dispatched parts of the 101st Airborne Division to restore order and uphold the Supreme Court's ruling.

Eisenhower may not have been as deeply committed to government intrusion into civil rights, but Faubus underestimated the president. The Constitution required that he enforce the laws of the land, and as executive he would do so. He might disagree with the law, but he would not defy it or his obligation as president.

As the nations' leader, Eisenhower had a duty to speak out on issues. By not doing so, he gave opponents a free hand and allowed them to think the president sympathized with them. By sending troops into Little Rock, Eisenhower gained praise for upholding the law of the land and for asserting the powers of the federal government, but by his silence he may have unwittingly lent encouragement to civil rights opponents. When Eisenhower was firmly committed to an issue, as he was in defeating Hitler, he supported it with every fiber. In this case, his commitment rested more with the duties of the executive than with civil rights.

Matters were different when it came to the state of the nation's highways. As far back as his 1919 expedition, Eisenhower understood the need for an adequate road network, a belief that was reinforced in World War II with his observation of the famed German autobahn. In 1956 he proposed what became the interstate highway system, the elaborate network of concrete that connected all sectors of the nation, sparked increased travel, and spurred the growth of restaurants and motels catering to vacationers. It is hard to think of a person who has not been affected by this underappreciated accomplishment: Eisenhower's plan made possible a quantum leap in the movement of people and products around the United States.

Eisenhower's eight years in office—the popular general easily won re-election in 1956, again over Adlai Stevenson—ended in January 1961. One of his final acts was to warn the nation of what he saw as an emerging danger. In his farewell address on January 17, he talked of the frightening power created by the convergence of the U.S. military with industry. He worried that in a democratic nation, too much power vested in one sector could be detrimental. "We must guard against the acquisition of unwarranted influence," he declared, "whether sought or unsought, by the military-industrial complex. The potential for the disastrous rise of misplaced power exists and will persist."[20]

Parallels extend into the twenty-first century. Books and Hollywood films have examined the possible role played by major oil companies in influencing events in the Mideast, and powerful industrial companies vie for rich military contracts in hardware and services. Eisenhower's warning in 1961 is as relevant now as it was in his time.

✦━═━✦

After leaving office in January 1961, Eisenhower and his wife returned to their family farm near Gettysburg. He wrote two presidential memoirs as well as his *At Ease: Stories I Tell to Friends,* and traveled to Normandy with newsman Walter Cronkite to commemorate the twentieth anniversary of D-Day.

The big heart that made Eisenhower unique among military men proved his undoing. During his years in the White House he had suffered a heart attack (1955) and a stroke (1957), but had recovered both times. A series of heart attacks beginning in 1965 left him so weakened that he spent the final year of his life in Walter Reed Army Hospital in Washington, D.C.

On March 28, 1969, the general and president succumbed, surrounded by the people he most loved—Mamie and his son. A few hours before he died, Eisenhower muttered to John, "I want to go; God, take me."[21]

CHAPTER 16

"There Is No Indispensable Man"

DWIGHT EISENHOWER WAS AN OUTSTANDING LEADER LONG BE-fore he supervised the campaign against Hitler. The qualities he exhibited, as early as his initial posting after his graduation from West Point, led to a spectacular career that culminated in two historic achievements—the defeat of Nazi Germany and the presidency.

Eisenhower enjoyed tremendous success because he rarely, if ever, varied from a set of principles that guided his command of people. He absorbed some of these principles from the men with whom he worked, such as Fox Conner. He developed others through trial and error as a young lieutenant and major.

After studying Eisenhower's career, one concludes that by the time he reached high command, where he directed armies and interacted with intimidating figures such as George Patton, Franklin D. Roosevelt, and Winston Churchill, five qualities guided his actions. While he employed the qualities in the military and political worlds, they can just as easily be used as lessons in leadership for any other arena, including business, science, or education. These qualities appeared throughout Eisenhower's career and affected the manner in which he responded to situations. They made Eisenhower a unique commander and most directly led to his success as a leader.

1. Focus

"His greatest claim to 'brilliance' rests on his utter relentlessness in the pursuit of his goal . . ."[1] wrote Eisenhower's son, John, in describing his father. Eisenhower early displayed a determination, whether it was in finishing first in his class at one of the Army command schools or in destroying Hitler. The business and sports worlds might divide this into two parts—setting goals, and then vigorously pursuing them. This quality marked Eisenhower's career from beginning to end.

His focus was most evident in World War II. He refused to veer from his broad-front strategy for the march across Europe, despite heavy pressures from Montgomery and Patton. At various times Eisenhower may have led his commanders to think he had agreed with them—thus opening himself to charges that he was too easily swayed—or endured what some considered unacceptable behavior, but that was his strategy to maintain the original plan. John Eisenhower observed this during one of his visits to his father's headquarters. "Time and again, Ike put up with the foibles, discourtesies, and downright arrogance of his official subordinate [in this case, Montgomery], while at the same time insisting that his major decisions be carried out."[2]

Eisenhower also refused to allow anyone or anything to nudge him from what he saw as the main objective of the war—to crush Hitler. Unlike in later American wars, such as Vietnam and Iraq, Eisenhower faced a definable foe, a clear evil whose destruction would terminate hostilities. Nothing deterred him from this mission, even though he faced intense pressure to alter his plans for political reasons. He was handed a task—the defeat of Hitler and the destruction of the German war machine—and within fifteen months he accomplished the monumental job.

Eisenhower clearly defined what he wanted before he started, and then used that goal as a moral and military compass to guide his actions through turmoil and triumph. He understood that the outcome mattered more than the details of the process to get there. George Marshall, in referring to criticism Eisenhower received during the fighting in North Africa, stated to Captain Harry Butcher, "If Rommel & Co. are tossed into the sea, all quibbling, political or otherwise, will be lost in the shouting of the major victory."[3] In three years, Eisenhower directed a team of planners who developed the precise strategy for the cross-channel operation, led an army onto the shores of France, sent it streaming across Western Europe, and annihilated one of the greatest armies in modern times.

Recent wars in American history have suffered in two ways—they have lacked a similar clarity of purpose, and they have not benefited from a convincing victory over a defined evil. Because Eisenhower had the first, he achieved the second.

2. Teamwork

"As much as possible within the framework of organization, I have always sought to develop a family feeling with my staff,"[4] Eisenhower stated in his memoirs. Throughout his career, he valued unity and teamwork above individual honors or glory. When superiors rebuked him and Patton for advocating an innovative use of the tank in the early 1920s, Eisenhower followed their wishes and moved on to his next assignment rather than complain. He detested MacArthur's love of dramatics and reacted bitterly when MacArthur tried to blame Eisenhower for the Philippine parade fiasco.

As a commander, Eisenhower expected fellow officers and staff members to express their thoughts on matters for his consideration. During the Louisiana maneuvers, for instance, he met daily with his officers to discuss the positives and negatives of the previous day's actions and the steps to improve them. In the tense days before D-Day, he gathered every senior commander at St. Paul's School, where he asked for their blunt assessments of the coming assault. Once he had sent the forces into action, he freely promoted his subordinates to the press rather than seek fame only for himself.

Eisenhower's team spirit extended especially to the soldier on the front line. When he commanded the 15th Infantry, he clearly explained his orders so that the men would understand what they were doing and why they did it. Eisenhower believed that this step led to improved performance, and he contended that in a democracy, such openness was essential. In England, he ordered that every American soldier be educated regarding the sacrifices their British brethren had endured so that they would better grasp the nature of the war.

During his 1945 speech in Guildhall, Eisenhower referred to the time when the first American troops arrived in London in 1942. "Most were mentally unprepared for the realities of war—especially as waged by the Nazis. Others believed that the tales of British sacrifice had been exaggerated. Still others failed to recognize the difficulties of the task ahead."

Eisenhower explained that after the Americans had been educated about the tribulations of their ally, relations vastly improved. "All such doubts, questions, and complacencies could not endure a single casual tour through your scarred streets and avenues . . . Gradually we drew closer together until we became true partners in war."[5]

His insistence on placing the team first led to victory over Germany in World War II. Despite being pulled in conflicting directions by heads of state and commanders from various nations, he kept the alliance intact. George Marshall wrote Eisenhower upon the war's conclusion that, "You have met and successfully disposed of every conceivable difficulty incident to varied national interests and international political problems of unprecedented complications."[6]

Even after the war, teamwork guided Eisenhower's actions. As the head of Columbia University, he prodded the institution to be "a more effective and productive member of the American national team,"[7] rather than isolate itself from other educational organizations, and he offered to work with his chief rival for the Republican nomination for president, Robert Taft, after defeating the senator.

Eisenhower may have stated it best. As he crossed the Atlantic Ocean aboard the *Queen Mary* with Mamie and other dignitaries to attend ceremonies marking the twentieth anniversary of D-Day, he took a piece of paper from his wallet to read to those assembled for dinner. The ending words summarize the general.

> "The moral of this quaint example
> Is to do just the best that you can.
> Be proud of yourself, but remember,
> There is no indispensable man."[8]

3. Empathy

"In the Army, whenever I became fed up with meetings, protocol, and paper work, I could rehabilitate myself by a visit with the troops. Among them, talking to each other as individuals, and listening to each other's stories, I was refreshed and could return to headquarters reassured that, hidden behind administrative entanglements, the military was an enterprise manned by human beings."[9]

The men on the line were a continual source of strength and encouragement to Eisenhower. After embarrassing a plebe at West Point, Eisenhower had vowed never to slight any man in his command, no matter what his rank. The incident aboard the transport to Panama, when he and Mamie had to surrender their quarters to two vacationing generals, reinforced this notion.

Eisenhower never forgot the infantryman under his care because he was one of them. His preferred casual gatherings to formal affairs; he preferred the great American pastimes of baseball and football to polo. He treated his men with the combination of stern, but fair, discipline, and bore no grudges to anyone who incurred his short-lived wrath. When his son, John, asked for advice as he began his military career, Eisenhower did not admonish him to study hard, to court favors from influential people, or to be fearless in battle. He told his son to take care of his men.

"He was constantly on the move," wrote Beetle Smith of Eisenhower, "visiting his subordinate commanders and talking with their troops . . ."[10] Eisenhower never forgot the individual American soldier, and that is the main reason they so loved him.

Eisenhower was intently concerned over the impact of his decisions on his men. Some commanders make decisions in a vacuum, moving armies and units about as if they were pieces on a game board. Others sent divisions and corps into battle; Eisenhower sent men. He recognized that while he issued commands in a comparatively safe, sheltered command post, somewhere on the line it resulted in a young soldier risking his life. The human factor in warfare was never far from his mind, perhaps because he had never assuaged his grief for Icky.

In his 1945 Guildhall address, Eisenhower said that a gifted commander might possess multiple talents, and his uniform might shine from the lustrous medals that bedecked it, but he "would sadly face the facts that his honors cannot hide in his memories the crosses marking the resting places of the dead. They cannot soothe the anguish of the widow or the orphan whose husband or father will not return." He added that, "Humility must always be the portion of any man who receives acclaim earned in blood of his followers and sacrifices of his friends."[11]

As president, Eisenhower attempted to put the arms race into perspective when he described the costs of a hydrogen bomb in terms of the schools or houses not constructed and warned of the perils of unrestricted nuclear development. "Science seems ready to confer upon us, as its final gift, the power to erase human life from this planet,"[12] he stated in his first speech as president.

In October 1944 he referred to the toll that death took on him when he wrote Mamie, "Just this minute there came to my desk a telegram announcing the death, in action, of the son of one of my best friends who is commanding an Army [the son of Lieutenant General Alexander M. Patch, commanding Seventh Army]. I must wire him at once. God, how wearying and wearing it all gets."[13] The suffering war caused was never far from Eisenhower's thoughts.

4. Media Savvy

This is an especially pertinent consideration in light of past developments in Vietnam and current ones in Iraq. The press in World War II did not as actively seek lurid headlines as do certain reporters today, but Eisenhower still showed a deft touch in managing what could have been a difficult group. If applied today, Eisenhower's tactics with the press in the 1940s could at least ameliorate the negatives of press coverage, for he treated them as allies rather than as adversaries. Eisenhower welcomed the press corps and worked with it as much as possible, for he understood that as much as they needed his viewpoint and information, he needed their help in conveying crucial messages to the American public and in the information the press could provide him.

"When secrecy had to be tightly observed," he wrote in his memoirs, "more than once I found that I could take correspondents into my confidence, telling them the full story of what was planned, and asking them to say or write nothing until the need for secrecy had ended. And the traffic of information was two-way: because they reflected far better than a military staff could the reactions of civilians at home and even of troops in combat, I learned much from them."[14]

Thus, in meetings with the press during the Louisiana maneuvers, he had imparted information about serious equipment shortages. He knew that once the information appeared in newspapers, it might so alarm the public that pressure from constituents would prod politicians to take appropriate steps. During the war, he appealed to the patriotism of three reporters in asking they suppress news of Patton's slapping incident. He convinced them that the nation would be better off with Patton commanding troops rather than idling away in some home-front training facility.

5. Devotion to Duty

This might seem to be a redundant quality to some, for should not devotion to duty be the reason all officers seek the military? It should, but frequently it is not. At numerous times in his life, Eisenhower showed that the call of duty governed his actions, not the summons of glory. Early in his career, he yearned to command soldiers in the field, but orders to staff positions crushed his hopes. Instead of complaining, he put aside his ambition and placed full effort into whatever task he faced. While most of his West Point classmates experienced combat in the fields of France in World War I, he labored at a string of training posts. As disappointed as he might have been, he declined lucrative financial offers on two occasions to remain in the military. His reasons simply stated were that he saw war coming and knew that the nation needed him.

Eisenhower was not one to act in his own interests, as MacArthur did in the Philippines or Montgomery and Patton did in Europe. He did what he was supposed to do as an army officer, even if it was not always what he wanted to do. As such he serves as a superb example for everyone.

These five qualities helped guide and define Eisenhower's life. Most likely, however, Mamie provided the best reason why her husband should be remembered—for "His honesty . . . integrity, and admiration for mankind."[15]

Notes

Introduction

1. Wallace C. Strobel, "The Picture," undated typewritten reminiscence of General Eisenhower's June 5, 1944, visit to the airborne troops, provided to the author, p. 1; author's interview with Wallace Strobel, December 1998.
2. Kay Summersby, *Eisenhower Was My Boss* (New York: Prentice-Hall, 1948), p. 146.
3. Strobel, "The Picture," p. 1.
4. Stephen E. Ambrose, *Eisenhower: Soldier, General of the Army, President-Elect, 1890–1952* (New York: Simon & Schuster, 1983), p. 309.
5. Eric Larrabee, *Commander in Chief: Franklin Delano Roosevelt, His Lieutenants, and Their War* (New York: Harper & Row, 1987), p. 455.
6. Geoffrey Perret, *Eisenhower* (Holbrook, Mass.: Adams Media, 1999), p. 282.
7. Strobel, "The Picture," p. 1.
8. Summersby, *Eisenhower Was My Boss*, p. 147.

Chapter 1

1. Dwight D. Eisenhower, *At Ease: Stories I Tell to Friends* (Garden City, NY: Doubleday, 1967), p. 30.
2. Carlo D'Este, *Eisenhower: A Soldier's Life* (New York: Henry Holt, 2002), p. 25.
3. D'Este, *Eisenhower: A Soldier's Life*, p. 39.
4. Geoffrey Perret, *Eisenhower* (Holbrook, Mass.: Adams Media, 1999), p. 34.
5. D'Este, *Eisenhower: A Soldier's Life*, p. 43.
6. Eisenhower, *At Ease: Stories I Tell to Friends*, pp. 41, 46.

7. Perret, *Eisenhower,* p. 33.
8. Eisenhower, *At Ease: Stories I Tell to Friends,* p. 37.
9. Perret, *Eisenhower,* p. 20.
10. Eisenhower, *At Ease: Stories I Tell to Friends,* p. 52.
11. D'Este, *Eisenhower: A Soldier's Life,* p. 18.
12. Daniel D. Holt and James W. Leyerzapf, eds. *Eisenhower: The Prewar Diaries and Selected Papers, 1905–1941* (Baltimore: Johns Hopkins University Press, 1998), p. 8.
13. Eisenhower, *At Ease: Stories I Tell to Friends,* p. 18.
14. Eisenhower, *At Ease: Stories I Tell to Friends,* p. 16.
15. D'Este, *Eisenhower: A Soldier's Life,* p. 83.

Chapter 2

1. Dwight D. Eisenhower, *At Ease: Stories I Tell to Friends* (Garden City, NY: Doubleday, 1967), p. 124.
2. Geoffrey Perret, *Eisenhower* (Holbrook, Mass.: Adams Media, 1999), p. 62.
3. Perret, *Eisenhower,* p. 65.
4. Eisenhower, *At Ease: Stories I Tell to Friends,* p. 119.
5. Eisenhower, *At Ease: Stories I Tell to Friends,* p. 133.
6. Stephen E. Ambrose, *Eisenhower: Soldier, General of the Army, President-Elect, 1890–1952* (New York: Simon & Schuster, 1983), p. 61.
7. Carlo D'Este, *Eisenhower: A Soldier's Life* (New York: Henry Holt, 2002), p. 124.
8. Eisenhower, *At Ease: Stories I Tell to Friends,* p. 136.
9. D'Este, *Eisenhower: A Soldier's Life,* p. 129.
10. Ambrose, *Eisenhower: Soldier, General of the Army, President-Elect,* p. 64.
11. Ambrose, *Eisenhower: Soldier, General of the Army, President-Elect,* p. 63.
12. Perret, *Eisenhower,* p. 70.

Chapter 3

1. Dwight D. Eisenhower, *At Ease: Stories I Tell to Friends* (Garden City, NY: Doubleday, 1967), p. 181.
2. Eisenhower, *At Ease: Stories I Tell to Friends,* pp. 181–182.
3. Carlo D'Este, *Eisenhower: A Soldier's Life* (New York: Henry Holt, 2002), p. 139.
4. Daniel D. Holt and James W. Leyerzapf, eds. *Eisenhower: The Prewar Diaries and Selected Papers, 1905–1941* (Baltimore: Johns Hopkins University Press, 1998), pp. 29, 34.
5. Eisenhower, *At Ease: Stories I Tell to Friends,* p. 173.
6. D'Este, *Eisenhower: A Soldier's Life,* p. 153.
7. Stephen E. Ambrose, *Eisenhower: Soldier, General of the Army, President-Elect, 1890–1952* (New York: Simon & Schuster, 1983), p. 77.

8. Eisenhower, *At Ease: Stories I Tell to Friends,* p. 185.
9. Eisenhower, *At Ease: Stories I Tell to Friends,* p. 187.

Chapter Four

1. Daniel D. Holt and James W. Leyerzapf, eds. *Eisenhower: The Prewar Diaries and Selected Papers, 1905–1941* (Baltimore: Johns Hopkins University Press, 1998), p. 139.
2. Carlo D'Este, *Eisenhower: A Soldier's Life* (New York: Henry Holt, 2002), p. 207.
3. Stephen E. Ambrose, *Eisenhower: Soldier, General of the Army, President-Elect, 1890–1952* (New York: Simon & Schuster, 1983), pp. 92–93.
4. D'Este, *Eisenhower: A Soldier's Life,* p. 224.
5. Dwight D. Eisenhower, *At Ease: Stories I Tell to Friends* (Garden City, NY: Doubleday, 1967), p. 214.
6. William Manchester, *American Caesar* (Boston: Little, Brown, 1978), p. 166.
7. John S. D. Eisenhower, *General Ike: A Personal Reminiscence* (New York: Free Press, 2003), pp. 20–21.
8. D'Este, *Eisenhower: A Soldier's Life,* p. 239.
9. Geoffrey Perret, *Eisenhower* (Holbrook, Mass.: Adams Media, 1999), p. 132.
10. D'Este, *Eisenhower: A Soldier's Life,* p. 239.
11. Eisenhower, *At Ease: Stories I Tell to Friends,* p. 226.
12. Robert H. Ferrell, ed., *The Eisenhower Diaries* (New York: W. W. Norton, 1981), p. 26.
13. Holt and Leyerzapf, *Eisenhower: The Prewar Diaries and Selected Papers, 1905–1941,* pp. 445–46.
14. Eisenhower, *At Ease: Stories I Tell to Friends,* p. 231.
15. D'Este, *Eisenhower: A Soldier's Life,* p. 250.

Chapter Five

1. Kenneth S. Davis, *Soldier of Democracy* (Garden City, NY: Doubleday, Doran, 1945), p. 257.
2. Carlo D'Este, *Eisenhower: A Soldier's Life* (New York: Henry Holt, 2002), p. 263.
3. Stephen E. Ambrose, *Eisenhower: Soldier, General of the Army, President-Elect, 1890–1952* (New York: Simon & Schuster, 1983), p. 122.
4. D'Este, *Eisenhower: A Soldier's Life,* p. 264.
5. D'Este, *Eisenhower: A Soldier's Life,* p. 263.
6. Daniel D. Holt and James W. Leyerzapf, eds. *Eisenhower: The Prewar Diaries and Selected Papers, 1905–1941* (Baltimore: Johns Hopkins University Press, 1998), pp. 465–66.
7. Holt and Leyerzapf, *Eisenhower: The Prewar Diaries and Selected Papers, 1905–1941,* pp. 508–9.

8. Holt and Leyerzapf, *Eisenhower: The Prewar Diaries and Selected Papers, 1905–1941,* p. 509.

9. Holt and Leyerzapf, *Eisenhower: The Prewar Diaries and Selected Papers, 1905–1941,* p. 545.

10. Ambrose, *Eisenhower: Soldier, General of the Army, President-Elect,* p. 124.

11. Holt and Leyerzapf, *Eisenhower: The Prewar Diaries and Selected Papers, 1905–1941,* p. 558.

12. Ambrose, *Eisenhower: Soldier, General of the Army, President-Elect,* p. 127.

13. D'Este, *Eisenhower: A Soldier's Life,* p. 269.

14. Dwight D. Eisenhower, *Crusade in Europe* (Garden City, NY: Doubleday, 1950), p. 11.

15. Ambrose, *Eisenhower: Soldier, General of the Army, President-Elect,* p. 129.

16. Davis, *Soldier of Democracy,* p. 272.

17. D'Este, *Eisenhower: A Soldier's Life,* p. 282.

18. Geoffrey Perret, *Eisenhower* (Holbrook, Mass.: Adams Media, 1999), pp. 143–44.

19. Eisenhower, *Crusade in Europe,* p. 14.

Chapter 6

1. Eric Larrabee, *Commander in Chief: Franklin Delano Roosevelt, His Lieutenants, and Their War* (New York: Harper & Row, 1987), p. 413.

2. Stephen E. Ambrose, *Eisenhower: Soldier, General of the Army, President-Elect, 1890–1952* (New York: Simon & Schuster, 1983), p. 134.

3. Robert H. Ferrell, ed., *The Eisenhower Diaries* (New York: W. W. Norton, 1981), p. 40.

4. Ferrell, *The Eisenhower Diaries,* p. 49.

5. Carlo D'Este, *Eisenhower: A Soldier's Life* (New York: Henry Holt, 2002), p. 295.

6. Stephen E. Ambrose, *The Supreme Commander: The War Years of General Dwight D. Eisenhower* (Garden City, NY: Doubleday, 1970), p. 18.

7. Ambrose, *The Supreme Commander,* pp. 21–22.

8. Ferrell, *The Eisenhower Diaries,* p. 47.

9. Ferrell, *The Eisenhower Diaries,* p. 49.

10. Ambrose, *Eisenhower: Soldier, General of the Army, President-Elect,* pp. 144–45.

11. Merle Miller, *Ike the Soldier: As They Knew Him* (New York: G. P. Putnam's Sons, 1987), p. 343.

12. D'Este, *Eisenhower: A Soldier's Life,* p. 301.

13. Winston Churchill, *The Second World War: Volume IV, The Hinge of Fate* (Boston: Houghton Mifflin, 1950), pp. 384–85.

14. Ambrose, *Eisenhower: Soldier, General of the Army, President-Elect,* p. 153.

15. Ferrell, *The Eisenhower Diaries,* p. 62.

16. In D'Este, *Eisenhower: A Soldier's Life,* p. 307.

Chapter 7

1. Robert H. Ferrell, ed., *The Eisenhower Diaries* (New York: W. W. Norton, 1981), p. 65.
2. Merle Miller, *Ike the Soldier: As They Knew Him* (New York: G. P. Putnam's Sons, 1987), p. 374.
3. Joseph Patrick Hobbs, ed., *Dear General: Eisenhower's Wartime Letters to Marshall* (Baltimore: Johns Hopkins Press, 1971), p. 25.
4. Stephen E. Ambrose, *Eisenhower: Soldier, General of the Army, President-Elect, 1890–1952* (New York: Simon & Schuster, 1983), p. 176.
5. Kay Summersby, *Eisenhower Was My Boss* (New York: Prentice-Hall, 1948), p. 8.
6. Michael R. Beschloss, *Eisenhower: A Centennial Life* (New York: HarperCollins, 1990), p. 41; Ambrose, *Eisenhower: Soldier, General of the Army, President-Elect,* p. 186.
7. Carlo D'Este, *Eisenhower: A Soldier's Life* (New York: Henry Holt, 2002), p. 332.
8. Dwight D. Eisenhower and John S. D. Eisenhower, ed., *Letters to Mamie* (Garden City, NY: Doubleday, 1978), p. 25, 38.
9. John S. D. Eisenhower, *General Ike: A Personal Reminiscence* (New York: Free Press, 2003), p. 12.
10. Ambrose, *Eisenhower: Soldier, General of the Army, President-Elect,* p. 179.
11. Beschloss, *Eisenhower: A Centennial Life,* p. 40.
12. Beschloss, *Eisenhower: A Centennial Life,* p. 40.
13. Summersby, *Eisenhower Was My Boss,* pp. 26, 28.

Chapter 8

1. Eric Larrabee, *Commander in Chief: Franklin Delano Roosevelt, His Lieutenants, and Their War* (New York: Harper & Row, 1987), p. 431.
2. Stephen E. Ambrose, *Eisenhower: Soldier, General of the Army, President-Elect, 1890–1952* (New York: Simon & Schuster, 1983), p. 199.
3. Ambrose, *Eisenhower: Soldier, General of the Army, President-Elect,* p. 204.
4. Dwight D. Eisenhower and John S. D. Eisenhower, ed., *Letters to Mamie* (Garden City, NY: Doubleday, 1978), p. 66.
5. Larrabee, *Commander in Chief: Franklin Delano Roosevelt, His Lieutenants, and Their War,* p. 435.
6. Harry C. Butcher, USNR, *My Three Years with Eisenhower* (New York: Simon & Schuster, 1946), p. 224.
7. Butcher, *My Three Years with Eisenhower,* p. 247.
8. Butcher, *My Three Years with Eisenhower,* p. 307.
9. Eisenhower, *Letters to Mamie,* pp. 94–95.
10. Larrabee, *Commander in Chief: Franklin Delano Roosevelt, His Lieutenants, and Their War,* p. 419.

11. Carlo D'Este, *Eisenhower: A Soldier's Life* (New York: Henry Holt, 2002), p. 383.
12. Butcher, *My Three Years with Eisenhower,* p. 263.
13. Butcher, *My Three Years with Eisenhower,* p. 265.
14. Rick Atkinson, *An Army at Dawn: The War in North Africa, 1942–1943* (New York: Henry Holt, 2002), p. 400.
15. Atkinson, *An Army at Dawn: The War in North Africa,* p. 477.
16. Dwight D. Eisenhower, *Crusade in Europe* (Garden City, NY: Doubleday, 1950), pp. 156–157.
17. Eisenhower, *Crusade in Europe,* p. 157.

Chapter 9

1. Dwight D. Eisenhower and John S. D. Eisenhower, ed., *Letters to Mamie* (Garden City, NY: Doubleday, 1978), p. 128.
2. Robert H. Ferrell, ed., *The Eisenhower Diaries* (New York: W. W. Norton, 1981), p. 111.
3. Carlo D'Este, *Eisenhower: A Soldier's Life* (New York: Henry Holt, 2002), p. 424.
4. Eisenhower, *Letters to Mamie,* p. 141.
5. Dwight D. Eisenhower, *Crusade in Europe* (Garden City, NY: Doubleday, 1950), p. 181.
6. Joseph Patrick Hobbs, ed., *Dear General: Eisenhower's Wartime Letters to Marshall* (Baltimore: Johns Hopkins Press, 1971), p. 121.
7. Alfred D. Chandler Jr., ed, *The Papers of Dwight David Eisenhower, The War Years: Volume III* (Baltimore: Johns Hopkins Press, 1970), pp. 1594–95.
8. Ferrell, *The Eisenhower Diaries,* p. 102.
9. Eisenhower, *Crusade in Europe,* p. 197.
10. James MacGregor Burns, *Roosevelt: The Soldier of Freedom* (New York: Harcourt Brace Jovanovich, 1970), p. 415.
11. Eric Larrabee, *Commander in Chief: Franklin Delano Roosevelt, His Lieutenants, and Their War* (New York: Harper & Row, 1987), p. 438.
12. Eisenhower, *Crusade in Europe,* p. 207.
13. Ferrell, *The Eisenhower Diaries,* p. 84.

Chapter 10

1. Stephen E. Ambrose, *Eisenhower: Soldier, General of the Army, President-Elect, 1890–1952* (New York: Simon & Schuster, 1983), p. 278.
2. Dwight D. Eisenhower, *Crusade in Europe* (Garden City, NY: Doubleday, 1950), p. 220.
3. Ambrose, *Eisenhower: Soldier, General of the Army, President-Elect,* p. 282.
4. Joseph Patrick Hobbs, ed., *Dear General: Eisenhower's Wartime Letters to Marshall* (Baltimore: Johns Hopkins Press, 1971), p. 162.

5. Ambrose, *Eisenhower: Soldier, General of the Army, President-Elect*, p. 283.
6. Omar N. Bradley, *A Soldier's Story* (New York: Henry Holt, 1951), p. 239.
7. Jon Meacham, *Franklin and Winston* (New York: Random House, 2003), p. 177.
8. Bradley, *A Soldier's Story*, p. 231.
9. Eisenhower, *Crusade in Europe*, p. 225.
10. Dwight D. Eisenhower and John S. D. Eisenhower, ed., *Letters to Mamie* (Garden City, NY: Doubleday, 1978), pp. 175–76.
11. Eisenhower, *Crusade in Europe*, p. 238.
12. Michael R. Beschloss, *Eisenhower: A Centennial Life* (New York: Harper-Collins, 1990), p. 41.
13. Hobbs, *Dear General: Eisenhower's Wartime Letters to Marshall*, p. 163.
14. Ambrose, *Eisenhower: Soldier, General of the Army, President-Elect*, p. 287.
15. Ambrose, *Eisenhower: Soldier, General of the Army, President-Elect*, p. 289.
16. Geoffrey Perret, *Eisenhower* (Holbrook, Mass.: Adams Media, 1999), pp. 274–75.
17. Eisenhower, *Crusade in Europe*, p. 246.
18. Robert H. Ferrell, ed., *The Eisenhower Diaries* (New York: W. W. Norton, 1981), pp. 119–20.
19. In Ferrell, *The Eisenhower Diaries*, p. 120.
20. Walter Bedell Smith, *Eisenhower's Six Great Decisions* (New York: Longmans, Green, 1956), p. 55.
21. Eisenhower, *Crusade in Europe*, p. 243.
22. Carlo D'Este, *Eisenhower: A Soldier's Life* (New York: Henry Holt, 2002), p. 1.

Chapter 11

1. Dwight D. Eisenhower, *Crusade in Europe* (Garden City, NY: Doubleday, 1950), p. 251.
2. Alfred D. Chandler Jr., ed, *The Papers of Dwight David Eisenhower, The War Years: Volume III* (Baltimore: Johns Hopkins Press, 1970), p. 1913.
3. Chandler, *Papers of Dwight David Eisenhower, The War Years: Volume III*, p. 1908
4. Harry C. Butcher, USNR, *My Three Years with Eisenhower* (New York: Simon & Schuster, 1946), p. 565.
5. Dwight D. Eisenhower and John S. D. Eisenhower, ed., *Letters to Mamie* (Garden City, NY: Doubleday, 1978), p. 190.
6. John S. D. Eisenhower, *General Ike: A Personal Reminiscence* (New York: Free Press, 2003), p. 115.
7. Stephen E. Ambrose, *Eisenhower: Soldier, General of the Army, President-Elect, 1890–1952* (New York: Simon & Schuster, 1983), p. 319.
8. Butcher, *My Three Years with Eisenhower*, p. 616.
9. Omar N. Bradley, *A Soldier's Story* (New York: Henry Holt, 1951), p. 371.
10. Walter Bedell Smith, *Eisenhower's Six Great Decisions* (New York: Longmans, Green, 1956), p. 63.

11. Bradley, *A Soldier's Story,* p. 376.
12. Eisenhower, *Crusade in Europe,* p. 279.
13. Butcher, *My Three Years with Eisenhower,* pp. 634–35.
14. Ambrose, *Eisenhower: Soldier, General of the Army, President-Elect,* p. 362.
15. Joseph Patrick Hobbs, ed., *Dear General: Eisenhower's Wartime Letters to Marshall* (Baltimore: Johns Hopkins Press, 1971), p. 195.
16. Robert H. Ferrell, ed., *The Eisenhower Diaries* (New York: W. W. Norton, 1981), p. 127.

Chapter 12

1. Peter Lyon, *Eisenhower: Portrait of the Hero* (Boston: Little, Brown, 1974), p. 306.
2. Alfred D. Chandler Jr., ed, *The Papers of Dwight David Eisenhower, The War Years: Volume III* (Baltimore: Johns Hopkins Press, 1970), p. 2100.
3. Dwight D. Eisenhower and John S. D. Eisenhower, ed., *Letters to Mamie* (Garden City, NY: Doubleday, 1978), p. 204.
4. Eisenhower, *Letters to Mamie,* p. 211.
5. John S. D. Eisenhower, *General Ike: A Personal Reminiscence* (New York: Free Press, 2003), p. 113.
6. Stephen E. Ambrose, *Eisenhower: Soldier, General of the Army, President-Elect, 1890–1952* (New York: Simon & Schuster, 1983), p. 316.
7. Geoffrey Perret, *Eisenhower* (Holbrook, Mass.: Adams Media, 1999), p. 312.
8. Lyon, *Eisenhower: Portrait of the Hero,* p. 295.
9. Carlo D'Este, *Eisenhower: A Soldier's Life* (New York: Henry Holt, 2002), p. 457.
10. Eric Larrabee, *Commander in Chief: Franklin Delano Roosevelt, His Lieutenants, and Their War* (New York: Harper & Row, 1987), p. 447.
11. Larrabee, *Commander in Chief: Franklin Delano Roosevelt, His Lieutenants, and Their War,* p. 479.
12. Kay Summersby, *Eisenhower Was My Boss* (New York: Prentice-Hall, 1948), p. 207.
13. Walter Bedell Smith, *Eisenhower's Six Great Decisions* (New York: Longmans, Green, 1956), p. 82.
14. Joseph Patrick Hobbs, ed., *Dear General: Eisenhower's Wartime Letters to Marshall* (Baltimore: Johns Hopkins Press, 1971), p. 199.
15. Alfred D. Chandler Jr., ed, *The Papers of Dwight David Eisenhower, The War Years: Volume IV* (Baltimore: Johns Hopkins Press, 1970), pp. 2143–44.
16. Dwight D. Eisenhower, *Crusade in Europe* (Garden City, NY: Doubleday, 1950), pp. 292–93.

Chapter 13

1. Merle Miller, *Ike the Soldier: As They Knew Him* (New York: G. P. Putnam's Sons, 1987), p. 717.

2. Kay Summersby, *Eisenhower Was My Boss* (New York: Prentice-Hall, 1948), p. 201.
3. Dwight D. Eisenhower, *Crusade in Europe* (Garden City, NY: Doubleday, 1950), p. 333.
4. Eisenhower, *Crusade in Europe*, pp. 333–34.
5. Robert H. Ferrell, ed., *The Eisenhower Diaries* (New York: W. W. Norton, 1981), p. 130.
6. Miller, *Ike the Soldier: As They Knew Him*, p. 719.
7. Charles B. MacDonald, *The Mighty Endeavor* (New York: Oxford University Press, 1969), p. 357.
8. Miller, *Ike the Soldier: As They Knew Him*, p. 720.
9. Geoffrey Perret, *Eisenhower* (Holbrook, Mass.: Adams Media, 1999), p. 327.
10. Ferrell, *The Eisenhower Diaries*, p. 130.
11. Perret, *Eisenhower*, p. 327.
12. Eisenhower, *Crusade in Europe*, p. 350.
13. Carlo D'Este, *Eisenhower: A Soldier's Life* (New York: Henry Holt, 2002), pp. 644–45.
14. D'Este, *Eisenhower: A Soldier's Life*, p. 653.
15. Dwight D. Eisenhower, *At Ease: Stories I Tell to Friends* (Garden City, NY: Doubleday, 1967), p. 291.
16. D'Este, *Eisenhower: A Soldier's Life*, p. 656.
17. D'Este, *Eisenhower: A Soldier's Life*, p. 657.
18. Perret, *Eisenhower*, p. 336.
19. D'Este, *Eisenhower: A Soldier's Life*, p. 657.
20. Eisenhower, *Crusade in Europe*, p. 356.
21. MacDonald, *The Mighty Endeavor*, p. 405.
22. Walter Bedell Smith, *Eisenhower's Six Great Decisions* (New York: Longmans, Green, 1956), p. 116.
23. Smith, *Eisenhower's Six Great Decisions*, p. 96.
24. Eisenhower, *At Ease: Stories I Tell to Friends*, p. 291.

Chapter 14

1. Dwight D. Eisenhower, *Crusade in Europe* (Garden City, NY: Doubleday, 1950), p. 369.
2. Walter Bedell Smith, *Eisenhower's Six Great Decisions* (New York: Longmans, Green, 1956), p. 146.
3. Stephen E. Ambrose, *Eisenhower: Soldier, General of the Army, President-Elect, 1890–1952* (New York: Simon & Schuster, 1983), p. 385.
4. Joseph Patrick Hobbs, ed., *Dear General: Eisenhower's Wartime Letters to Marshall* (Baltimore: Johns Hopkins Press, 1971), p. 220.
5. Omar N. Bradley, *A Soldier's Story* (New York: Henry Holt, 1951), p. 511.
6. Dwight D. Eisenhower and John S. D. Eisenhower, ed., *Letters to Mamie* (Garden City, NY: Doubleday, 1978), p. 245.

7. Eisenhower, *Crusade in Europe,* p. 406.
8. Eisenhower, *Letters to Mamie,* p. 244.
9. Hobbs, *Dear General: Eisenhower's Wartime Letters to Marshall,* p. 216.
10. Carlo D'Este, *Eisenhower: A Soldier's Life* (New York: Henry Holt, 2002), p. 680.
11. Smith, *Eisenhower's Six Great Decisions,* p. 136.
12. Hobbs, *Dear General: Eisenhower's Wartime Letters to Marshall,* p. 226.
13. Eisenhower, *Crusade in Europe,* p. 389.
14. Hobbs, *Dear General: Eisenhower's Wartime Letters to Marshall,* p. 223.
15. Eisenhower, *Letters to Mamie,* p. 248.
16. Ambrose, *Eisenhower: Soldier, General of the Army, President-Elect,* p. 398.
17. Hobbs, *Dear General: Eisenhower's Wartime Letters to Marshall,* pp. 221–22.
18. Smith, *Eisenhower's Six Great Decisions,* p. 221.
19. Smith, *Eisenhower's Six Great Decisions,* pp. 182–86.
20. D'Este, *Eisenhower: A Soldier's Life,* p. 692.
21. D'Este, *Eisenhower: A Soldier's Life,* p. 695.
22. Smith, *Eisenhower's Six Great Decisions,* p. 229.
23. Smith, *Eisenhower's Six Great Decisions,* pp. 206–7.

Chapter 15

1. Dwight D. Eisenhower, *At Ease: Stories I Tell to Friends* (Garden City, NY: Doubleday, 1967), p. 299.
2. John S. D. Eisenhower, *General Ike: A Personal Reminiscence* (New York: Free Press, 2003), p. 206.
3. Douglas Kinnard, *Eisenhower: Soldier-Statesman of the American Century* (Washington, D.C.: Brassey's, 2002), p. 57.
4. Carlo D'Este, *Eisenhower: A Soldier's Life* (New York: Henry Holt, 2002), p. 4.
5. Eisenhower, *At Ease: Stories I Tell to Friends,* p. 301.
6. Geoffrey Perret, *Eisenhower* (Holbrook, Mass.: Adams Media, 1999), p. 359.
7. Eisenhower, *At Ease: Stories I Tell to Friends,* p. 324.
8. Eisenhower, *At Ease: Stories I Tell to Friends,* pp. 342–43.
9. Michael R. Beschloss, *Eisenhower: A Centennial Life* (New York: Harper-Collins, 1990), p. 93.
10. Tom Wicker, *Dwight D. Eisenhower* (New York: Henry Holt, 2002), p. 10.
11. Wicker, *Dwight D. Eisenhower,* p. 13.
12. Max Hastings, *The Korean War* (New York: Touchstone, 1987), p. 317.
13. Hastings, *The Korean War,* p. 326.
14. Wicker, *Dwight D. Eisenhower,* p. 60.
15. Eisenhower, *General Ike: A Personal Reminiscence,* p. 108.
16. Kinnard, *Eisenhower: Soldier-Statesman of the American Century,* p. 67.
17. Wicker, *Dwight D. Eisenhower,* p. 23
18. Wicker, *Dwight D. Eisenhower,* p. 129.

19. Wicker, *Dwight D. Eisenhower,* p. 47.
20. Wicker, *Dwight D. Eisenhower,* p. 132.
21. Kinnard, *Eisenhower: Soldier-Statesman of the American Century,* p. 97.

Chapter 16

1. John S. D. Eisenhower, *General Ike: A Personal Reminiscence* (New York: Free Press, 2003), p. 218.
2. Eisenhower, *General Ike: A Personal Reminiscence,* pp. 219–20.
3. Harry C. Butcher, USNR, *My Three Years with Eisenhower* (New York: Simon & Schuster, 1946), p. 278.
4. Dwight D. Eisenhower, *At Ease: Stories I Tell to Friends* (Garden City, NY: Doubleday, 1967), p. 322.
5. Eisenhower, *General Ike: A Personal Reminiscence,* p. 225.
6. Stephen E. Ambrose, *Eisenhower: Soldier, General of the Army, President-Elect, 1890–1952* (New York: Simon & Schuster, 1983), p. 408.
7. Ambrose, *Eisenhower: Soldier, General of the Army, President-Elect,* p. 482.
8. Carlo D'Este, *Eisenhower: A Soldier's Life* (New York: Henry Holt, 2002), p. 705.
9. Eisenhower, *At Ease: Stories I Tell to Friends,* p. 343.
10. Walter Bedell Smith, *Eisenhower's Six Great Decisions* (New York: Longmans, Green, 1956), p. 221.
11. Eisenhower, *General Ike: A Personal Reminiscence,* pp. 223–24.
12. Geoffrey Perret, *Eisenhower* (Holbrook, Mass.: Adams Media, 1999), p. 521.
13. Dwight D. Eisenhower and John S. D. Eisenhower, ed., *Letters to Mamie* (Garden City, NY: Doubleday, 1978), p. 217.
14. Eisenhower, *At Ease: Stories I Tell to Friends,* p. 321.
15. Douglas Kinnard, *Eisenhower: Soldier-Statesman of the American Century* (Washington, D.C.: Brassey's, 2002), p. 98.

Bibliography

Ambrose, Stephen E. *Eisenhower: Soldier, General of the Army, President-Elect, 1890–1952.* New York: Simon & Schuster, 1983.

_____. *The Supreme Commander: The War Years of General Dwight D. Eisenhower.* Garden City, NY: Doubleday, 1970.

Atkinson, Rick. *An Army at Dawn: The War in North Africa, 1942–1943.* New York: Henry Holt, 2002.

Beschloss, Michael R. *Eisenhower: A Centennial Life.* New York: HarperCollins, 1990.

Bradley, Omar N. *A Soldier's Story.* New York: Henry Holt, 1951.

Burns, James MacGregor. *Roosevelt: The Soldier of Freedom.* New York: Harcourt Brace Jovanovich, 1970.

Butcher, Harry C. *My Three Years with Eisenhower.* New York: Simon & Schuster, 1946.

Chandler, Alfred D., Jr., ed. *The Papers of Dwight David Eisenhower, The War Years: Volumes I-V.* Baltimore: Johns Hopkins Press, 1970.

Churchill, Winston. *The Second World War: Volume IV, The Hinge of Fate.* Boston: Houghton Mifflin, 1950.

Davis, Kenneth S. *Soldier of Democracy.* Garden City, NY: Doubleday, Doran, 1945.

D'Este, Carlo. *Eisenhower: A Soldier's Life.* New York: Henry Holt, 2002.

Eisenhower, Dwight D. *Crusade in Europe.* Garden City, NY: Doubleday, 1950.

_____. *At Ease: Stories I Tell to Friends.* Garden City, NY: Doubleday, 1967.

Eisenhower, Dwight D., and John S. D. Eisenhower, ed. *Letters to Mamie.* Garden City, NY: Doubleday, 1978.

Eisenhower, John S.D. *General Ike: A Personal Reminiscence.* New York: Free Press, 2003.

Ferrell, Robert H., ed. *The Eisenhower Diaries.* New York: W.W. Norton, 1981.

Hastings, Max. *The Korean War.* New York: Touchstone, 1987.

Hobbs, Joseph Patrick, ed. *Dear General: Eisenhower's Wartime Letters to Marshall.* Baltimore: Johns Hopkins Press, 1971.

Holt, Daniel D., and James W. Leyerzapf, eds. *Eisenhower: The Prewar Diaries and Selected Papers, 1905–1941.* Baltimore: Johns Hopkins University Press, 1998.

Kinnard, Douglas. *Eisenhower: Soldier-Statesman of the American Century.* Washington, D.C.: Brassey's, 2002.

Larrabee, Eric. *Commander in Chief: Franklin Delano Roosevelt, His Lieutenants, and Their War.* New York: Harper & Row, 1987.

Lash, Joseph P. *Eleanor and Franklin.* New York: W.W. Norton, 1971.

Leckie, Robert. *Delivered From Evil: The Saga of World War II.* New York: Harper & Row, 1987.

Lyon, Peter. *Eisenhower: Portrait of the Hero.* Boston: Little, Brown, 1974.

MacDonald, Charles B. *The Mighty Endeavor.* New York: Oxford University Press, 1969.

Manchester, William. *American Caesar.* Boston: Little, Brown, 1978,

Meacham, John. *Franklin and Winston.* New York: Random House, 2003.

Miller, Merle. *Ike the Soldier: As They Knew Him.* New York: G.P. Putnam's Sons, 1987.

Perret, Geoffrey. *Eisenhower.* Holbrook, Mass.: Adams Media, 1999.

Smith, Walter Bedell. *Eisenhower's Six Great Decisions.* New York: Longmans, Green, 1956.

Strobel, Wallace C. "The Picture." Undated typewritten reminiscence of General Eisenhower's June 5, 1944, visit to the airborne troops.

Summersby, Kay. *Eisenhower Was My Boss.* New York: Prentice-Hall, 1948.

Wicker, Tom. *Dwight D. Eisenhower.* New York: Henry Holt, 2002.

Index